Prentice-Hall, Inc., Englewood Cliffs, N.J.

Modernization:

Protest

and

Change

S. N. EISENSTADT The Hebrew University
Jerusalem

Library of Congress Catalog Card No.: 66-22805

Current printing (last digit):

10   9   8   7   6   5   4   3   2

Printed in the United States of America
C-55940(P)   C-55941(C)

PRENTICE-HALL INTERNATIONAL, INC.
London

PRENTICE-HALL OF AUSTRALIA, PTY. LTD.
Sydney

PRENTICE-HALL OF CANADA, LTD.
Toronto

PRENTICE-HALL OF INDIA (PRIVATE) LTD.
New Delhi

PRENTICE-HALL OF JAPAN, INC.
Tokyo

WILBERT E. MOORE / NEIL J. SMELSER   Editors

Modernization of Traditional Societies Series

The twentieth century will be called many
things by future historians—the Age of Global
War, perhaps, the Age of Mass Society,
the Age of the Psychoanalytic Revolution,
to name a few possibilities. One name that
historians certainly will not fail to give
our century is the Age of the New Nation. For,
evidently, the convulsive emergence of
the colonies into independence and their
subsequent struggle to join the ranks of the
prosperous, powerful, and peaceful is the
most remarkable revolution of our time.
Taking the world as a whole, men are now
preoccupied with no subject more than they
are with the travail of the New Nations.
The world of the social sciences
has been studying the pace of social
change in these newly emergent areas,
and from time to time has been engaging in
technical assistance and even in the giving
of advice on high levels of social strategy.
Little of this effort has reached publicly
accessible form. Though technical treatises
abound, and isolated, journalistic reports
of distinctly exotic countries are not
wanting, college curricula have scarcely
reflected either the scientific endeavors or
the world-wide revolutions in technology
and in political affairs.
This series on "Modernization of
Traditional Societies" is designed to
inform scholars, students, and citizens about
the way quiet places have come alive, and
to introduce at long last materials on
EDITORIAL FOREWORD the contemporary character of

developing areas into college curricula for the thought leaders of the near future. To these ends we have assembled experts over the range of the social sciences and over the range of the areas of the underdeveloped and newly developing sections of the earth that were once troublesome only to themselves.

We are proud to be participants in this series, and proud to offer each of its volumes to the literate world, with the hope that that world may increase, prosper, think, and decide wisely.

WILBERT E. MOORE
NEIL J. SMELSER

This book attempts to present a sociological approach to problems of modernization in general and of political modernization in particular through an analysis of the major characteristics and problems of modern and modernizing societies. The focal point of this approach is that the major problem facing such societies is the necessity to develop an institutional structure which is capable of continuously "absorbing" the various social changes which are inherent in the processes of modernization and the different degrees of ability to do so which can be found in different societies. The major concern of the book is to understand the conditions under which modernizing and modern societies develop such an institutional framework as against conditions in which there develop cases of "breakdown" or "regression" of modernization.

Such analysis, however, has to face the fact of the great structural variety of modern societies, the ways in which such variety may be connected, perhaps to conditions of sustained growth as against conditions of breakdown. The second part of the book therefore deals with the analysis of different patterns of modernization as they have developed in some modern and modernizing societies. This analysis is of necessity very brief and presupposes some minimal knowledge about their historical and contemporary settings. It attempts to provide some insights which might be of some

value for both the specialists in the study

of these societies and for those interested in comparative analysis.

The book does not pretend to give answers to the many questions it raises. One of its major goals is to raise such questions and only indicate the beginnings of possible answers—beginnings which might be useful for further analysis—which will go far beyond the tentative answers presented here.

This book is an outgrowth of a longstanding concern of mine with the problems of development and modernization—a concern which is still continuing and which might hopefully lead to more detailed analyses of various aspects and problems of modernization.

Perhaps the most important stage in the development of this concern came in the year 1962-63, which I spent as Carnegie Visiting Professor of Political Sciences at M.I.T. It was there, through my contacts with Harold Isaacs, Dan Lerner, Lucien Pye, Ithiel de Sola Pool, Myron Wiener, and Robert Wood, as well as with colleagues at Harvard, and especially Talcott Parsons and Robert N. Bellah, that the orientations presented here gradually crystallized.

My greatest debt in the study of modernization in general and in the preparation of this book in particular I owe to Edward Shils, whose work in this field has greatly inspired my own, who has indeed developed some of the crucial concepts used here—such as that of "consensual mass society" and "center and periphery"—and who was also good enough to go over in very great detail several parts of the book and to improve them considerably.

I would also like to thank Professor A. Diamant of Haverford College, Professor E. Gellner of the London School of Economics, Professors M. Confino and Jacob Katz of the Hebrew University, and Professor Neil Smelser of the University of California, Berkeley, who read drafts of the book and made very useful criticisms. I also thank Dr. R. Bar-Yoseph for reading part of the manuscript and Mrs. R. Shaco for her help with the proofs.

A large part of the research and travel connected with my work on modernization has been supported by the Rockefeller Foundation to whom I would like to express my gratitude.

S. N. EISENSTADT

CHAPTER ONE   **The Basic Characteristics
of Modernization**   **1**

The Background   1
Social Mobilization and Social Differentiation   2
Continuous Structural Differentiation and Changes   5
Organizational and Status Systems   7
The Political Field   11
Consensual Mass Tendencies of Modern Societies   15
The Educational Field   16
International Aspects of Modernization   18

CHAPTER TWO   **Social Disorganization,
Transformation, and Protest in Modernization**   **20**

Social Change, Disorganization, and Structural Dislocation   20
The Consequences of Disorganization   22
Social Problems and Social Policy   25
The Changing Pattern of Youth Problems   26
Structural Change and Orientations of Protest   31
The Major Themes of Social Protest   32
The Major Themes of Cultural Protest   34
International Aspects of Protest   35

CHAPTER THREE   **Structural Change, Structural
Diversity, and Problems of
Sustained Growth in Modernization**   **36**

Orientations of Protest, Structural Change, and
Integrative Problems   36
Development of Change-Absorbing Institutions   38
System Transformation and Sustained Growth   40
Structural Diversity   43
Different Historical Starting Points and
Orientations of Modernizing Elites   46
Structural Diversity and Conditions of Sustained Growth   49

Contents

CHAPTER FOUR **Patterns Developing in the First Phase of Modernization** **51**

Introduction 51
Patterns of Continuous, Pluralistic Modernization in Western Europe, the United States and the Dominions 55
The Modernizing Elites and Orientations 55
Temporal Sequence and Structural Characteristics of Modernization 58
Absorption of Change in the Pluralistic-Constitutional Regimes 59
Movements of Protest and Patterns of Eruptions 61
France and Italy—Some Comparative Notes 65
The Spread of Modernization Beyond Western Europe 67
The Development of Split-up Modernization 67
Autocratic Regimes—Germany and Russia 69
Temporal Sequence and Structural Characteristics in Split-up Modernization 72
Patterns of Absorption of Change 73
Orientations of Protest and Patterns of Eruption 74
The Process of Modernization in Japan 75
Modernization under a Revolutionary Oligarchy 75
Temporal Sequence and Structural Characteristics of Modernization 78
The Political Process and Absorption of Change 79
The Breakdown of the Japanese System in the Thirties 81

CHAPTER FIVE **Patterns Developing in the Second Phase of Modernization** **83**

Characteristics of Societies in the Second Stage of Modernization 83
Patterns of Modernization in Latin America 84
The Initial Pattern 84
Structural Changes and Structural Duality 86
Elite Formation and Structural Duality 90
Structural Duality and Breakdowns 94
Differences among Latin American Countries 96
Revolutionary-nationalist and Communist Regimes 98
Common Characteristics of the Revolutionary Regimes 98
Structural Characteristics of Nationalistic-revolutionary Regimes 102
Growing Differentiation and New Orientations of Protest 104

Specific Characteristics of the Communist Regimes   105
Absorption of Change and Orientations of Protest   107
The Transformation of Colonial Societies   109
Initial Modernizing Orientations of Colonial Powers   109
Unbalanced Change in Colonial Societies   111
The Repercussion of Unbalanced Change in
the Political Sphere   112
Transformation of Modernizing Attitudes   115
Basic Structural Characteristics of
Centers and Periphery   116
Stratification and Ideology   118
Major Problems of Integration   120
Some Major Differences among the New States   124

CHAPTER SIX   **A Comparative Analysis of
Situations of Breakdown and
of Sustained Growth   129**

The Ubiquity of Eruptions in Modern Societies   129
Possible Outcomes of Eruptions   131
Characteristics of Situations of Breakdown   133
Movements of Protest   135
Processes of Communication   136
Cleavages between Elites   137
Contractual Arrangements and Precontractual Symbols   140
Characteristics of Political Process in
Situations of Sustained Growth   142

CHAPTER SEVEN   **Preliminary Conclusions: Conditions
of Breakdown and of Sustained Growth   145**

Introduction   145
Interrelations between Elites and Broader Strata   147
Structural Flexibility: The Political Field   149
Rigidity and Flexibility of Status Systems   151
Some Conditions of Structural Flexibility   154
Ideological Transformation and Cohesion of Elites   156
Formations and Orientations of Elites in
Situations of Breakdown   159

Index   162

Modernization and aspirations to modernity are probably the most overwhelming and the most permeating features of the contemporary scene. Most nations are nowadays caught in its web—becoming modernized or continuing their own traditions of modernity. As it spreads throughout the world, its common features as well as the differences between its characteristics in various countries stand out—and it is the purpose of this book to explore and analyze these common features and differences alike. Historically, modernization is the process of change towards those types of social, economic, and political systems that have developed in western Europe and North America from the seventeenth century to the nineteenth and have then spread to other European countries and in the nineteenth and twentieth centuries to the South American, Asian, and African continents.

Modern or modernizing societies have developed from a great variety of different traditional, premodern societies. In western Europe they developed from feudal or absolutist states with strong urban centers, in eastern Europe from more autocratic states and less urbanized societies. In the United States and the first Dominions (Canada, Australia, etc.) they have developed through processes of colonization and immigration, some of which were rooted in strong religious motivations and organized in groups of religious settlers,

CHAPTER ONE

The Basic Characteristics of Modernization

1

while others were based mostly on large-scale immigration oriented mostly to economic opportunity and greater equality of status.

In Latin America more fragmentarily modern structures developed from oligarchic conquest-colonial societies, in which there existed strong division between the white conquering oligarchy and the indigenous subject population. In Japan the modernization process developed from a centralized feudal state of somewhat unique characteristics and in China from the breakdown of the most continuous Imperial system in the history of mankind, a system based on special types of "literati-bureaucratic" institutions.

In most Asian and African societies the process of modernization has begun from within colonial frameworks, some (especially in Asia) based on preceding more centralized monarchical societies and elaborate literary-religious traditions, others (especially in Africa) mostly on tribal structures and traditions.

As we shall see, the different starting points of the processes of modernization of these societies have greatly influenced the specific contours of their development and the problems encountered in the course of it. And yet beyond these variations there also developed many common characteristics which constitute perhaps the major core of "modernization" of a modern society, and it would be worth while to analyze these characteristics.

SOCIAL MOBILIZATION AND SOCIAL DIFFERENTIATION

The common characteristics of modernization refer both to what may be called socio-demographic aspects of societies and to structural aspects of social organization.

Karl Deutsch has coined the term "social mobilization" to denote most of the socio-demographic aspects of modernization.[1] He has defined social mobilization as "the process in which major clusters of old social, economic and psychological commitments are eroded and broken and people become available for new patterns of socialization and behavior," and has indicated that some of its main indices are exposure to aspects of modern life through demonstrations of machinery, buildings, consumers' goods, etc.; response to mass media; change of residence; urbanization; change from agricultural occupations; literacy; growth of per capita income, etc. (These in themselves do not indicate, of course, whether the resources made available in this way will indeed be mobilized.)

Modern societies are also highly differentiated and specialized with respect to individual activities and institutional structures. Recruitment

[1] K. W. Deutsch, "Social Mobilization and Political Development," *American Political Science Review*, 55 (September 1961), 494-95.

to these is not determined in characteristically modern societies in any fixed, ascriptive kinship, territorial caste, or estate framework. The specialized roles are "free-floating" (i.e., admission to them is not determined by ascribed properties of the individual); similarly wealth and power are not ascriptively allocated—at least not as much as in nonmodern societies. This is associated with institutions like markets in economic life, voting and party activities in politics, and instrumentally recruited bureaucratic organizations and mechanisms in most institutional spheres.[2]

Perhaps the most important aspects of this differentiation and specialization of roles in all the major institutional spheres is the *separation* between the different roles held by an individual—especially among the occupational and political roles, and between them and the family and kinship roles. This separation has taken place first, and perhaps most dramatically, between family and economic occupational roles during the industrial revolution, as has been so fully described by Marx in his studies of the Industrial Revolution and the emergence of the industrial system, by Tönnies in his classical studies of "Community and Society," and by Simmel in his studies of urban life.[3]

Such separation of roles meant, first, that the occupation of any given role within one institutional sphere—e.g., the occupational sphere—does not automatically entail the incumbency of a particular role in the political or cultural spheres. Second, within each institutional sphere (in the economy, polity, in the sphere of social organization, etc.) there developed distinctive units that were organized around the goals specific to each such sphere and that were not fused, as in more traditional societies, with other groups in a network based on family, kinship, and territorial bases.

In the economic sphere proper these developments have been characterized by the development of a very high level of technology (based on and combined with Newtonian science), fostered by the systematic application of knowledge, the pursuit of which became the province of specialized scientific institutions, and by the secondary (industrial, commercial) and tertiary (service) occupations, as against the primary extractive ones. In other words, by the development of industrial sys-

[2] On these aspects of modernization, see T. Parsons, *Structure and Process in Modern Societies* (New York: Free Press of Glencoe, Inc., 1959), Chaps. 3, 4; D. Lerner, *The Passing of Traditional Society* (New York: Free Press of Glencoe, Inc., 1958); B. F. Hoselitz, "Noneconomic Factors in Economic Development," *American Economic Review*, 47 (May 2, 1957), 28-71; and J. A. Kahl, "Some Social Concomitants of Industrialization and Urbanization," *Human Organization*, 18, 2 (Summer 1959), 53-75.

[3] G. Simmel, "The Metropolis and Mental Life," in P. Hatt and A. Reiss, eds., *Cities and Society* (New York: Free Press of Glencoe, Inc., 1957); and F. Tönnies, *Community and Association*, trans. Charles P. Loomis (London: Routledge & Kegan Paul, Ltd., 1955).

tems based on high level of technology, on growing specialization of economic roles and of units of economic activity—production, consumption, and marketing—and on the growth of the scope and complexity of the major markets, the markets for goods, labor, and money.[4]

In the political sphere modernization has been characterized, first, by growing extension of the territorial scope and especially by the intensification of the power of the central, legal, administrative, and political agencies of the society. Second, it has been characterized by the continual spread of potential power to wider groups in the society— ultimately to all adult citizens, and their incorporation into a consensual moral order.

Third, modern societies are in some sense democratic or at least populistic societies. They are characterized by the decline of traditional legitimation of the rulers with reference to powers outside their own society (God, reason) and by the establishment of some sort of ideological accountability, usually also institutional, of the rulers to the ruled, who are alleged to be the holders of the potential political power.

All these characteristics are, of course, connected with the greater fluidity of political support, with the large degree of "interest-oriented," nonideological political allegiance and with considerable weakening, sometimes almost total disappearance, of ascriptive political commitment to any given ruler or group. Thus the rulers, in order to maintain themselves effectively in power and receive support for the specific goals they propagate and the policies they want to implement, believe they must seek continually the political support of the ruled, or at least of large or vocal parts thereof, through elections, plebiscites, and acclamatory surrogates.[5]

Unlike the rulers of traditional autocratic regimes, the rulers of the totalitarian regimes accept the relevance of their subjects as the objects and beneficiaries, legitimators of policy. The difference between modern democratic or semi-democratic and totalitarian political systems lies not necessarily in the genuineness of these beliefs, but in the extent to which they are given institutional expression in pluralistic political organizations, in public liberties, and in welfare and cultural policies.[6]

In the cultural sphere, a modern society is characterized by a growing differentiation of the major elements of the major cultural and value

[4] W. Moore, "The Social Framework of Economic Development," in R. Braibanti and J. Spengler, eds., Tradition, Values and Socio-Economic Development (Durham, N.C.: Duke University Press, 1961), pp. 57-82.

[5] S. N. Eisenstadt, "Bureaucracy and Political Development," in J. La Polambara, ed., Bureaucracy and Political Development (Princeton, N.J.: Princeton University Press, 1963), pp. 96-120.

[6] S. N. Eisenstadt, "Political Modernization: Some Comparative Notes," International Journal of Comparative Sociology, 5, 1 (March 1964), 3-24.

systems, i.e., religion, philosophy, and science; the spread of literacy and secular education; a more complex intellectual institutional system for the cultivation and advancement of specialized roles based on intellectual disciplines.[7]

These developments have been very closely related to the expansion of media of communication, the growing permeation of such central media of communication into the major groups of the society, and the wider participation of these groups in the cultural activities and organizations created by the centrally placed cultural elites.[8]

The culmination of these developments has been the development of a new cultural outlook—perhaps the most pervasive aspect of modernization—even though its spread and permeation has been, in these societies, intermittent and very uneven. This outlook has been characterized by an emphasis on progress and improvement, on happiness and the spontaneous expression of abilities and feeling, on individuality as a moral value, and concomitant stress on the dignity of the individual and, last, on efficiency.[9] This has been manifest in the development of some new personality orientations, traits, and characteristics—greater ability to adjust to the broadening societal horizons; some ego-flexibility; widening spheres of interest; growing potential empathy with other people and situations; a growing evaluation of self-advancement and mobility; and a growing emphasis on the present as the meaningful temporal dimension of human existence.[10]

CONTINUOUS STRUCTURAL DIFFERENTIATION AND CHANGES

In the societies that have made the journey, the movement to modernity has passed through a certain sequence of stages. Thus, to take the political field at different stages of the development of modern political systems, different problems became politically important and different types of political organization tended to develop. At certain stages of modernization, the problem of suffrage, of the definition of the new political community, of attainment of its independence, assumed central importance. In other societies or at other stages, problems of religious toleration or of so-called secularization of culture were most prominent. In still other stages of modernization the economic and

[7] E. Shils, "Political Development in New States," *Comparative Studies in History and Society* (Spring–Summer 1960), 265-92, 379-411; and K. Mannheim, *Man and Society in an Age of Reconstruction* (London: Routledge & Kegan Paul, Ltd., 1940).

[8] Mannheim, *ibid.;* and L. Pye, ed., *Communication and Political Development* (Princeton, N.J.: Princeton University Press, 1963).

[9] Lerner, *op. cit.*

[10] Shils, *op. cit.;* and A. Inkeles, "Industrial Man: The Relation of Status to Experience, Perception and Value," *American Journal of Sociology,* 66, 1 (July 1960), 1-31.

social problems were most pertinent. The development of each of these problems was necessarily connected with the entrance of different new groups and strata into the political arena.

Similarly, new types of political organization have been developing. From small and parliamentary cliques, from varied, relatively restricted but fully articulated interest groups on the one hand, and from different types of social movements on the other, there developed more fully organized political parties—the mass parties. Later, especially in Europe and the United States from the late twenties on, the relative importance of such parties and of the legislatures in which they were prominent became to some extent smaller, giving rise to more extensive and fully organized interest groups, on the one hand, and to the growing importance of the executive and administrative branches of the government, and especially to large-scale bureaucratic administration, on the other.[11]

In the economic sphere we witness the transition from relatively small-scale units of production, such as family firms, small factories, and commercial and banking enterprises operating for relatively restricted, local markets, to the more centralized, bureaucratized, and larger units of production such as the big corporations, trusts, cartels operating in more encompassing, large-scale new markets. Similarly, new techniques of production that greatly affected the structure of the economic process have been continually developing, giving rise to a growing and more complicated division of labor *within* each unit on the one hand and to growing complexity of the general market structure on the other.[12]

In the occupational system we witness, first, the continual development of new categories and groups. In the first stages of modernization the occupational structure might have been relatively uncomplicated and composed mostly of different manual occupations, unskilled and skilled, a small number of "middle-class" occupations, such as trade and manufacture, and of some of the more traditional professions such as the ecclesiastical (religious), military, legal, and medical ones, including a much smaller proportion of population. Later, with continued economic development, each of these categories became divided into many subcategories. In addition, many new groups and categories—welfare service, scientific, technological, managerial—emerged and increased.[13]

The very development of new, more complex units of production, within each of which there increased the number of different categories of occupational manpower (i.e., technical, professional, administrative),

[11] Shils, *ibid.;* and Eisenstadt, *op. cit.*
[12] W. E. Moore, *The Impact of Industry* (Englewood Cliffs, N.J.: Prentice-Hall, Inc., 1965); and C. S. Belshaw, *Traditional Exchange and Modern Markets* (Englewood Cliffs, N.J.: Prentice-Hall, Inc., 1965).
[13] Parsons, *op. cit.*

has also given a push to the rise of new types of professional occupations and associations. These were no longer limited to the traditional professions—law, medicine, etc.—but spread out also to other occupational categories, such as scientific and technological research, nursing, social work, and business and managerial positions. In most of these one can discern a growing trend to professionalization, i.e., to the demand for higher educational qualifications as a prerequisite for engaging in them, on the one hand, and to some autonomous self-regulatory organization on the other. These developments tended to obliterate or weaken many of the older distinctions between different occupations.[14] They also give rise to continual new types of trade union organization and to different patterns of labor-workers' relations. From the relatively simple union limited mostly to one factory, locality, or industrial branch, there developed the country-wide unions organized in different types of federations. These have spread into white- and blue-collar occupations, creating within each new problems and demands. Hence the relations between the different units of production or consumption became enmeshed in a growing number of crosscutting allegiances and contacts between new organizations composed of different subgroups within each of these units.

In the demographic-ecological sphere we witness a continuous trend to the weakening of small, local rural and urban units in which any given population could take care of most of its needs within relatively narrow ecological confines.

The performance of such different functions—housing, work, schooling, entertainment, etc.—becomes more and more dispersed between different and far-apart ecological areas. At the same time there developed growing metropolitan areas within which new ecological subunits tended to develop.[15]

ORGANIZATIONAL AND STATUS SYSTEMS

The characteristic features of the associational structure of modern society are, first, the large number of functionally specific organizations; second, the division of labor between functionally specific and more solidary or culturally oriented associations; and third, the weakening of the importance of the kinship and narrow territorial bases of specialized associations on the one hand, and of various "specialized" associations and broad ascriptive-solidary groups on the other.[16]

[14] Moore, *The Impact of Industry.*
[15] D. V. Glass, *The Town in a Changing Civilization* (London: John Lane, 1935); Simmel, *op. cit.;* and L. Wirth, "Urbanism as a Way of Life," in Hatt and Reiss, eds., *op. cit.,* pp. 46-63.
[16] M. Weber, "Class, Status, Party," in H. Gerth and C. W. Mills, eds., *From Max Weber* (London: Routledge & Kegan Paul, Ltd., 1947), pp. 180-95.

This structural differentiation had several repercussions in the area of social stratification, the most important of which is the development of an ambiguous status system.[17] The tendency found in many premodern societies for most property, power, and status relations either to coalesce or to be segregated in a rather rigid hierarchical order, tends to break down with the process of modernization. This could be seen first in the high importance of criteria of universalism and achievement in all major institutional spheres. The social position held by anyone in different social spheres were no longer necessarily identical and there was no necessary coalescence between them. One's place in the political or "social" sphere was not as assured as in many premodern societies by virtue of one's economic or occupational standing; or vice versa. While strong tendencies to some such coalescence exist in all modern societies, they are usually counteracted as a result of the relative independence of the different distribution of people in these different spheres.

This mobility in modern societies is not only that of individuals and families moving between relatively given and fixed structural positions. There is also a creation of new structural positions, as a result of new types of business enterprise, labor organization, or political or administrative organization, and of new criteria of evaluation of such positions.

Closely related to the preceding characteristics has been the development of new types of mechanisms of regulation and allocation of social roles and activities.[18] These mechanisms may be analyzed first in terms of the scope of their operation, i.e., distinguishing between relatively small-scale and large-scale fields of regulation. Second, they can be analyzed according to the nature of the criteria of allocation which develop in them; first, "who" allocates or integrates different roles and facilities; and second, how the process of allocation, regulation, and consequent integration is organized or structured.

As for the first, one can distinguish between ascriptive and nonascriptive allocation or regulation. Ascriptive allocators or regulators are those who perform such roles by virtue of their "given," usually hereditary, position in some groups, such as kinship, territorial, or estate groups. The nonascriptive regulators are characterized by the fact that they occupy their positions by virtue of some achieved position—either by being chosen to represent other people or groups, or by virtue of their ownership of special capital, or of some specific knowledge expertise.

[17] M. Tumin, "Competing Status Systems," in W. Moore and A. Feldman, eds., *Labor Commitment and Social Change in Developing Areas* (New York: Social Science Research Council, 1960), pp. 277-88; and L. Fallers, "Equality, Modernity and Democracy in the New States," in Clifford Geertz, ed., *Old Societies and New States* (New York: Free Press of Glencoe, Inc., 1963), pp. 158-219.

[18] Mannheim, *op. cit.;* and C. Kerr, *Industrialism and Industrial Man* (Cambridge, Mass.: Harvard University Press, 1960).

Second, we may distinguish between direct and indirect allocation—according to the extent of the directness of the interaction between the allocator and his "clients."

The most general characteristic of organizational developments in modern society has been the continual weakening of ascriptive and direct allocation and regulation, and the development of various mechanisms of nonascriptive and indirect allocation.

There are three such major types of mechanisms. One is the representative or public type, in which the principles of allocation are established by the public deliberation of "representatives" of various types of constituencies. Political representatives, voluntary associations, and professional organizations are the most important examples of this type of mechanism. Second are the various impersonal market systems such as the labor market or the markets for money and commodities. The third major type is the bureaucratic type, characterized by regulation by "experts" or by people whose major qualification is some specific knowledge, either general administrative or more specific professional or technical knowledge. These experts are in turn supervised to some extent by holders of political, economic, or communal power, but only to very little extent *directly* by the clients to whom they provide their services. The "ideal type" of bureaucratic regulation stresses the "rational," computative allocation and decision making which is worked out "rationally" according to the exigencies of any given situation and belittles allocation by elected representatives, by organs of self-government, through processes of political or legislative decision or by exigencies of the "impersonal" mechanisms of the market.

Another very important aspect of the system of stratification that tended to develop with processes of modernization was the growing dissociation between *elite and broad status groups* (strata, classes), and among the different elites themselves.

In all these spheres there have been developed categories of groups or of people whose members are leaders in various institutional spheres, without at the same time being confined to members of definite strata or classes. This applies to the bureaucrats, the economic entrepreneurs, the military, the intellectuals, and the different political elites alike.[19]

Such distinctive elite groups developed not only in the central levels of political and cultural activity, but also, in a somewhat different way, in what may be called the local levels. Political, cultural, economic, and social (community) leadership in the middle and lower urban strata and in various rural settings was no longer entirely a matter of traditional hereditary positions.

[19] See S. N. Eisenstadt, "Bureaucracy, Bureaucratization, Markets and Power Structure," in *Essays in Comparative Institutions* (New York: John Wiley & Sons, Inc., 1965), pp. 175-216.

But if, on the one hand, the different elite groups became continuously dissociated from broader status groups and more autonomous, on the other hand there took place a continuous differentiation among the elites themselves. One such important differentiation was that between elites oriented to more general, collective or cultural, diffuse goals and activities that focused on the promotion of various symbols of solidarity—such as the political and intellectual (especially the literary, journalistic) on the one hand and the more specialized elites, such as various professional, technical, or managerial ones, on the other. Of no smaller importance was the growing differentiation within each of these broad types of elites.[20]

The relative importance of such different modernizing elites has varied from society to society and within the same society at different stages of its development, and such relative importance may have greatly influenced, as we shall see, the course of the process of modernization in any society. But whatever the differences between different societies, the common characteristics outlined above tended to develop, in varying degrees, in all modern and modernizing societies.

These developments in the field of social organization have also been closely related to a growing dissociation between institutionalized and formal institutions on the one hand, and relatively smaller primary groups on the other.[21] In many premodern societies there existed a relatively high degree of coalescence between the more institutionalized and the more informal and solidary (very often ecological and kinship) units, although, of course, such coalescence was never full. Village councils and medieval guilds are perhaps the best examples of such coalescence. With the onset of modernization such coalescence tended to weaken. In most institutional spheres there continued to develop many formal, large-scale organizations cutting across various ecological, kinship, and castlike groups. Within these large-scale frameworks there tended to develop many different, mostly informal solidary primary groups, such as those of factory workers or of chance neighbors—groups that were not fully institutionalized or very closely interwoven into the broader, more formalized organizations.[22]

The most important single "external" ecological manifestation of these changes has been the process of urbanization, the conglomeration of parts of the population in urban centers in which the more specialized types of economic, professional, and civic activities and enterprises became concentrated and expanded.

[20] Mannheim, op. cit.

[21] E. Shils, "The Study of the Primary Group," in D. Lerner and H. Lasswell, eds., The Policy Sciences (Stanford, Calif.: Stanford University Press, 1951), pp. 44-70.

[22] Fallers, op. cit.

The process of urbanization has usually been very closely related to the breakdown of at least some of the more traditional ascriptive criteria of status, whether tribal, estate, or regional ones, and to the development of somewhat more flexible and variegated social strata; to the upsurge of social mobility through occupational, educational, and political channels; and to the development of a great variety of forms of social organization, ranging from various functionally specific economic enterprises to various civic and voluntary associations and professional groups.

All these processes—the dissociation between functionally specific groups and broader solidarities, between the criteria of status, between social strata and elites, and between formal and informal aspects of social organization—have created a status system of great fluidity and ambiguity. The assurance of a fixed given position which spilled over most of an individual's institutional roles was being continually undermined. It was undermined not only by personal or family fortunes or misfortunes but by the very nature of the system of social organization, by the continual changes and structural differentiation. Hence, although these developments usually opened up new perspectives of advancement and change of status, status necessarily became also a focus of insecurity, awareness, and political conflict.[23]

THE POLITICAL FIELD

The process of modernization has been characterized not only by continuous structural differentiation in the major institutional spheres of the society, however. Side by side with this process there also occurred the breakdown of the self-sufficiency and closeness of different groups and strata, as they were drawn toward a more unified, common institutional and societal center, and began to impinge on the central institutional and symbolic sphere of the society.

The various subgroups, be they local units, status groups, or traditional vocational or professional bodies, have been drawn together into common institutional and organizational frameworks. In the economic sphere it was manifest in the development of encompassing markets and widespread bureaucratic organizations. In the field of social organization and stratification it was manifest in the various aspects of the associational structure analyzed above, and in the fact that different social groups and strata became more and more aware of each other's standing in terms of power, prestige, and wealth, and began to measure themselves and other groups in terms of relatively similar values and standards.

[23] T. Parsons, *Societies in Comparative and Evolutionary Perspectives*, forthcoming.

Whatever the exact details of this process of drawing wide groups into the central institutional spheres of the society, they all epitomize the growth and concretization of the demand for equality. By virtue of the drawing of various groups into the central institutions of the society equality has become not just an abstract ideal but an overwhelming demand for growing concrete participation of all groups in all spheres of life.[24]

Let us illustrate in somewhat greater detail these processes of drawing of the wider social groups into the central institutional spheres in two areas—the political and the educational. As in all other political systems, so in the modern ones, the rulers have to deal both with "objective" problems, such as international relations, economic conditions, mobilization of economic resources, and with mobilization of political support. But the connection between these two aspects of the political process became much more close and interwoven in the modern than in other types of political systems. The growing participation of wider strata of population in the political struggle makes these groups much more sensitive and interested in—although not necessarily always better able to understand—these "objective" problems.

Similarly, the process of articulation of political demands and activities in modern political systems is much more closely related to the provision of resources to the political elite than in other types of political system. The effective political organization of the ruled is here almost a basic prerequisite of the continual provision of resources to the central political institutions. Because of this the availability—at different levels—of elites that are able to mobilize resources and political support and at the same time to articulate political demands is of crucial importance for the working of these systems. This is evident in the fact that the major organ of articulation of political interests and of mobilization of political support for the rulers—the party—also becomes an important organ of a crucial area of policy and decision making.[25]

Among the specific types of organization through which political demands are articulated, of special importance are interest groups, social movements, and "public opinion" and political parties.[26] The first three may to some extent be seen as components of the last, i.e., of parties that are the most articulate forms of modern political organization; moreover, there may exist considerable overlapping between them, yet

[24] E. Shils, "Centre and Periphery," in The Logic of Personal Knowledge, essays presented to Michael Polanyi (London: Routledge and Kegan Paul, 1961).

[25] Eisenstadt, "Political Modernization: Some Comparative Notes"; and W. Kornhauser, The Politics of Mass Society (New York: Free Press of Glencoe, Inc., 1959).

[26] G. Almond, "Introduction: A Functional Approach to Comparative Politics," in G. Almond and J. S. Coleman, eds., The Politics of Developing Areas (Princeton, N.J.: Princeton University Press, 1960), pp. 3-64.

all of them have some autonomous existence and orientations of their own.

The interest or pressure group is usually oriented to the gaining of concrete, specific interests, be they economic, religious, cultural, or political, and is interested in the wider, broader political machinery of the party or of the state only insofar as it can directly promote this interest, or at least assure its optimal promotion in a given situation. There are, of course, many diverse types of such interest groups—economic, professional, religious, ethnic, or tribal—and their specific interests may vary greatly from situation to situation.

The second type of organization through which political orientations and demands are articulated in modern political systems is social movements.[27] Several types of such movements can be distinguished. One is the relatively restricted movement oriented to the attainment of some specific general goal that is not directly related to a concrete interest of any articulate group but represents the application of some wider principle of justice—such as movements against capital punishment, for improvement of the lots of deprived groups or of categories of people (unmarried mothers, delinquents, etc.), for abolition of slavery, etc. The second type is the reform movement, which aims at some change in the central political institutions, such as extension of suffrage to some group. These two types of movement often constitute important ingredients of public opinion, to be discussed shortly.

The third and most extreme and specific type of social movement is the ideological, totalistic one, which usually aims at development of some new total society or polity. It attempts to infuse inclusive and diffuse values or goals into a given institutional structure or to transform such a structure according to these aims and values. It usually has a strong "future" orientation and tends to depict the future as greatly different from the present, and to fight for the realization of this change. It very often contains some apocalyptical, semi-Messianic elements, and it tends usually to make demands of total obedience or loyalty on its members and to make extreme distinctions between friends and foes.

The third element through which political demands are articulated in modern political systems is what has been called "general, diffuse, intelligent interest in public issues and in the public good." [28] By this is meant people or groups who have a rather more flexible attitude to

[27] H. Cantril, *The Psychology of Social Movements* (New York: John Wiley & Sons, Inc., 1941); and H. Kohn, "Pan-Movements," in *Encyclopaedia of the Social Sciences* (New York: The Macmillan Company, 1933), xi, pp. 544-54.

[28] C. J. Friedrich, *Constitutional Government and Democracy* (rev. ed.) (New York: Blaisdell Publishing Co., 1950); and Eisenstadt, "Political Modernization: Some Comparative Notes."

both specific interests and to "total" ideas and claims, who are not firmly attached to any given interest group, movement, or organization, and whose main concern is for the general public good and in the sober evaluation of a political program in terms of both general values and concrete possibilities.

Many elements—including some of the orientations of movements and interest groups—may enter into the formation of public opinion, and yet the diffuse public opinion tends to crystallize in patterns of its own, specified above.

Each of these forms of articulation of interests has existed in various forms in premodern systems also, but with several differences.[29] One such difference is that with the partial exception of petitions or entreaties by interest groups or cliques, the representation of the political activities and orientations of groups was not, in premodern societies, fully legitimized within the central political institutions, while social or social-religious movements were largely a-political or nonlegitimate from the point of view of the existing political institutions.

A second difference is that these groups were mostly concerned with petitioning the rulers for various concrete benefits and not with determining major political goals or selecting of rulers. A third is rooted in the fact that it is only in the modern political system that these different interest groups and movements may become integrated, even if only to a small extent, into the framework of common continuous political activity and organization, such as political parties, or other organizations that perform similar functions of mobilization of support and of integration of different political demands. Such integration is attained by the parties (or other partylike organizations) through the development of specific party organs, leadership, and programs; through the subsumption within the party of various concrete interests under some more general rules or aims that may be of some appeal to a wider public; and through the translation, as it were, of the inclusive, diffuse aims of the social movements into more realistic terms of concrete political goals, issues, and dilemmas, articulated through some party or partylike organizations and activities.

The exact ways and combinations between these different types of political demands tend to vary greatly, as we shall see in greater detail later, in different modern regimes.

Similarly, at different stages of the development of modern political systems, there have developed, as mentioned above, different problems that became important, and different types of organizational frameworks through which such problems were dealt with. Thus at certain stages

[29] S. N. Eisenstadt, *The Political Systems of Empires* (New York: Free Press of Glencoe, Inc., 1963).

of modernization, the problem of suffrage and of the definition of the new political community, of attainment of its independence, assumed most central importance. In other spheres or at other stages, problems of religious toleration or of so-called secularization of culture were most prominent, while in still other stages of modernization the economic and social problems as well as problems of organization were pertinent. The development of each of these problems was necessarily connected with the entrance of different new groups and strata into the political arena.[30]

Perhaps the most important aspect of this process is that within any modern political system new problems and forms of political organization tend to develop continually and new groups are continually drawn into the central political orbit; and that their problems, interests, and demands tend more and more to impinge on the central political institutions, on the selection of rulers, on the creation and crystallization of central political symbols, and on the choice and implementation of different major policies.

The broader strata of society tend more and more to impinge on its central institutions, not only in making various demands on it but also in the sense of developing the aspirations to participate in the very crystallization of the center, its symbols, and its institutional contours. The major social movements that have developed with the onset of modernization, national, social, or cultural, all manifest in varying degrees and intensity this tendency to growing participation of broader strata in the central sphere of the society.

CONSENSUAL MASS TENDENCIES OF MODERN SOCIETIES

The preceding analysis brings out perhaps the most central characteristics of modern societies—their basic mass-consensual orientation.[31]

The consensual or mass aspect of modern society is rooted in the growing impingement of broader strata on the center, in their demands to participate in the sacred symbols of society and their formulation, and in the deplacement of the traditional symbols by new ones that stress these participatory and social dimensions.

This tendency to broad, mass consensuality does not, of course, find its fullest institutionalized expression in all different types of modern societies. In many regimes in the first stages of modernization it may be weak or intermittent, while totalitarian regimes of course tend to suppress its fullest expression. But even totalitarian regimes attempt to legitimize themselves in terms of such values, and it is impossible to

[30] S. M. Lipset, *Political Man* (Garden City, N.Y.: Doubleday & Company, Inc., 1960).
[31] E. Shils, "The Theory of Mass Society," *Diogenes*, 39 (1963), 45-66.

understand their policies, their attempts to create symbols of mass consensus, without assuming the existence of such consensual tendency among the major strata within them and its acknowledgement by the rulers.

The culmination of all these developments has been the crystallization of the nation and nation-state as the most important socio-political unit of modern societies, and of the possibility of a civil order as the major type of socio-political order within it.[32]

The nation and the nation-state emerged as the most common new sovereign political unit and focus of collective political and cultural identity. The symbols of common national social and cultural identity were no longer chiefly traditional, defined in terms of restricted tribal, traditional, or status groups. Although the new national symbol usually had a distinct territorial referent, and often a kinship, it was much more abstract and mythical and much less traditional and included many more subgroups of various kinds. Among many strata there developed some measures of differentiated, but not rigidly ascribed, identification with common cultural symbols that were neither entirely limited to any one territorial or kinship unit nor mediated by it. This is very closely related to the tendency to the establishment of the civil order, an order in which all citizens, irrespective of kinship, status, or territorial belonging, participate and share the same set of central institutions.

The growing participation of broader strata in the center of the society and in the civil order can be seen as two basic attributes of modern nation-building, of the establishment of new, broader political and social entities, whose symbols of identity are couched in nontraditional terms and whose institutional frameworks cut across narrower parochial units and emphasize more general, universalistic criteria.[33]

THE EDUCATIONAL FIELD

Perhaps the best starting point for the analysis of the characteristics in the educational institutions in modern societies is the pattern of demands for and the supply of educational services that tended to develop with modernization.[34] These were greatly influenced by the attempts of various groups to attain new goals in various fields of social life, by the demands for manpower made by developing economic structure, and by the attempts made by various elite groups to influence the educational process, either as means of political influence and social

---

[32] E. Shils, "Primordial, Personal, Sacred and Civil Ties," *British Journal of Sociology,* 8 (June 1957), 130-46.

[33] E. Kedourie, *Nationalism* (London: Hutchinson & Co. (Publishers), Ltd., 1961).

[34] S. N. Eisenstadt, *Education and Political Development,* Duke University Commonwealth Seminar Series (Durham, N.C.: Duke University Press, 1962-63).

control or for the assurance of economic manpower. In the field of demand we can distinguish between the demand for the "products" and the "rewards" of education. Among the most important products of education are, first, various skills, be they general skills, such as literacy, which are assumed to be good preparation for a great variety of occupations, or more specific professional and vocational skills, the number of which has continually increased and become diversified with growing economic, technical, and scientific development.

A second major product of education is identification with various cultural socio-political symbols and values and of relatively active commitment to various cultural, social, and political groups and organizations.

The different social groups—economic and administrative entrepreneurs and organizations, different political, social, and cultural elites, parties, groups, and the more dispersed and diffuse orientations of citizens in general and of parents in particular—exerted different and continually changing demands for the "products" and "rewards" of education, such as different economic rewards, preparation for different occupations and occupational advancement, and preparation for social mobility or for affirmation of status position, as well as for participation in the wider social, political, and cultural affairs and movements.

The supply side of educational services also became greatly diversified and differentiated. It included on the one hand the supply of the manpower to be educated at different levels of the educational system, and adequate motivation and preparation for education. On the other hand, it included the supply of various schooling facilities—schools at different levels, ranging from kindergartens to universities, of teaching personnel (greatly dependent on fluctuation in the labor market), and of various facilities for the maintenance of such institutions and organizations. These could be supplied by the government and by various elites and entrepreneur groups, in the center of the society and on different local levels.

Out of the interaction of these varied pressures there developed the basic structural characteristics of educational institutions or systems in modern societies.

Among these characteristics, the most important were the growing specialization of educational roles and organizations, on the one hand, and growing unification and interrelation of the different educational activities within the frameworks of one common system on the other. The educational activities and organizations tended to become more widespread and a continuous differentiation between the different levels of the educational system—between primary, secondary, vocational, adult, and higher education—took place. Each of these "systems," and even many subsystems of each, has gradually become more autonomous, specialized, and organized in its own framework. On the other hand, however, these different organizations became more closely interconnected either through some overall educational planning or through the fact that one became a recognized channel for advancement into the other, as well as through the growing competition between them for the same manpower and resources.[35]

But this bringing together of the various types of educational activities within one common institutional framework did not necessarily assure any harmony or identity between the various aspects of the process of supply and demand for educational activities and products. On the contrary, the possibility of some discrepancy between these different aspects was inherent in the very nature of their interaction. But these discrepancies continually brought together various groups of the population into common frameworks, increasing their interdependence on the one hand and their pressures on the central institutional sphere of the society on the other.

INTERNATIONAL ASPECTS OF MODERNIZATION

Historically, the first processes of modernization, those of western and central Europe, have developed from within a social order that was characterized by the existence of multiplicity of different political units sharing the same cultural heritage. While modernization has in many ways disrupted many aspects of this order, in other ways it only accentuated the identification with this common cultural heritage and intensified the relations between the new emerging political units.[36]

From the very beginning the process of modernization was not confined within separate national or "state" communities. The major economic trends and developments and the major social and cultural movements which developed with the onset of modernization, such as the various social and political movements, cut across national or political boundaries. The nationalistic movements of the nineteenth and twentieth centuries themselves were, paradoxically perhaps, international in scope and orientation.

Many of the specifically modern social groups and elites—such as religious and intellectual groups or entrepreneurial firms—developed close relations cutting across existing and emerging political boundaries. Moreover, the very spread of modernization from its initial upsurge in western Europe was to no small degree due to the concomitant development of a new type of international system or systems. The development of the first modern national states—England, France, the Netherlands, and the

[35] J. Floud and A. Halsey, "The Sociology of Education: A Trend Report and Bibliography," *Current Sociology*, 7 (1958), 165-235.
[36] D. Thomson, *Europe since Napoleon* (New York: Alfred A. Knopf, Inc., 1962).

Scandinavian states—created a challenge to the more "traditional" rulers of central, eastern, and southern Europe, and later of the Middle East— to set on a program of limited (mostly technical) modernization that would enable them to stand on their own in the new international framework. On the other hand these very attempts of the rulers, as well as the increasing flow of communication between these societies, has created within these societies many new elite groups, which tend to establish relations with similar groups in other countries, creating in a way an international system of their own within which new impetus—often in opposition to those of the rulers—tend to develop.[37]

In the first stages of modernization these various international trends converged mostly around problems of formation and crystallization of national communities and symbols. Later, in contemporary Europe and to some extent in Latin America and Africa, when the process of social and economic differentiation or of political interrelationships began more and more to cut across older units, many new concrete economic and organizational (and not only symbolic) frameworks tend to arise and processes and problems of interstate integration become more important. Thus the boundaries of the overall political communities that tended to crystallize into the processes of modernization were not fixed or given, but tended to change in different periods or stages of modernization.

[37] E. Shils, "The Intellectual and the Powers: Some Perspectives for Comparative Analysis," *Comparative Studies in Society and History*, 1, 1 (1958), 5-23.

The very fact that modernization entails continual changes in all major spheres of a society means of necessity that it involves processes of disorganization and dislocation, with the continual development of social problems, cleavages and conflicts between various groups, and movements of protest, resistance to change.[1]

Disorganization and dislocation thus constitute a basic part of modernization, and every modern and modernizing society has to cope with them. These processes have two closely related aspects—that of disorganization proper of the existing patterns of life of various groups, and that of growing interconnection between different groups undergoing these processes, of their being brought together into common frameworks, and of their mutual impingement on one another.

The continuous process of urbanization, of migration from the countryside to urban centers, has often disorganized both rural communities and the older types of urban setting, and has created, especially in its initial phases, many manifestations of social disorganization and sheer misery.

deskilly

[1] On the development of social problems, see S. N. Eisenstadt, ed., *Comparative Social Problems* (New York: Free Press of Glencoe, Inc., 1964), *passim.* On the development of cleavages, see S. M. Lipset, *Political Man* (Garden City, N.Y.: Doubleday & Company, Inc., 1960).

CHAPTER TWO

Social Disorganization, Transformation, and Protest in Modernization

The processes of industrialization have continually been disrupting the older patterns of work and production, have made many of the older skills redundant, and have diminished the traditional security (even if this was a security on a very low level of subsistence) associated with many traditional occupations in agriculture and handicrafts. These processes have put large parts of the population at the vagaries of the labor markets and have created unemployment or underemployment as a perennial problem of industrial society, on a larger scale than the perennial Lumpenproletariat of traditional cities.

Each new stage of industrialization—the transition from the "first" to the "second" Industrial Revolution, the transition to automation in many of contemporary societies—has continually recreated these problems in new forms.

These varied developments have impinged on the field of the family, have decreased the scope of its activities and functions and fostered tension and alienation between the generations, to an extent probably unprecedented in any other society. They have also created various forms of delinquency, crime, and vagrancy, which have tended to develop together with the disorganization of the traditional patterns of ecological, community setting and of the family.

The process of political centralization and democratization, of the extension of political equality, has undermined the status and standing of older elites and holders of power positions, and has modified various traditional loyalties toward these elites and the importance of many of the intermediary bodies (such as various groups of notables or traditional local and professional organizations).

The processes of cultural modernization, which include secularization, have weakened the certainty of the accepted, long-established values and traditions and of their bearers and representatives. They have created, on the one hand, the possibility of continual competition among diverse cultural elites within each national group or in the modern world as a whole, in the creation of new values, symbols, traditions, and cultural activities, and in their transition to broader groups. On the other hand, the democratization of cultural opportunities and moral equalitarianism here helped to open the way for "mass culture," i.e., for a culture in which strata excluded from the "high culture" of society respond positively to cultural products that are looked down upon by those who continue the high cultural tradition.

Both the political and the cultural processes attendant on modernization have paradoxically enough created, through the very drawing in of broader groups to the center, the potential for alienation of wide groups from the central political and social system, for the development of feelings of anonymity and anomic estrangement from their societies, which became stronger as their expectation of participation in the center given grew.

All these processes have, however, created not only various loci of disorganization but have also increased the mutual interdependence and impingement of major groups and strata; hence, also the possibility of conflicts among them. The bringing together of various groups and strata into relatively common frameworks, and the growing interaction between them, could greatly increase the cleavages and conflicts among them. Different groups became more dependent on each other and more aware of one another, which served not only to broaden the areas of conflicts between them and multiply their number, but to enhance their perception and intensity.

The very processes analyzed above in relation to social disorganization have also been very closely connected with the possibility of growing cleavages and conflicts. As industrialization and urbanization have of necessity increased the scope of conflicts between different groups and classes, so the extension of political participation has brought together, into the political arena, many new groups with potentially conflicting interests.

The trend to the integration of wider strata in the central spheres of the society has inevitably tended to exacerbate the importance of these new conflicts and cleavages and to enhance their potential importance within the total society.

Conflicts of interest between different groups and strata—between peasants and landlords, artisans and merchants, slaves and slave-owners —have existed, of course, in all societies. But it is only in modern societies, with the drawing together of the different groups into the central spheres of society, that these conflicts have become centralized, unifying potentially opposing camps, facilitating their society-wide organization, their becoming symbols of social and political identification, and their making demands on the central political institution.[2]

THE CONSEQUENCES OF DISORGANIZATION

The processes of disorganization on the one hand, and of mutual impingement of the major groups and strata on the other, posed important problems for the emerging modern social institutions and frameworks.

Perhaps the most general manifestation of disorganization proper can be found in the continual growth of areas in which "social problems" developed.[3] Social problems are usually designated as breakdowns

[2] E. Durkheim, *The Division of Labour in Society* (New York: Free Press of Glencoe, Inc., 1947); and W. Kornhauser, *The Politics of Mass Society* (New York: Free Press of Glencoe, Inc., 1959).

[3] Eisenstadt, ed., *op. cit.*

or deviations of social behavior, involving a considerable number of people, which are of serious concern to many members of the society in which the aberrations occur. They tend to arise especially in those areas of social life in which the more formal institutional arrangements and demands impinge on the more spontaneous or basic, primordial aspects or attributes of individuals and communities. As such they become perhaps especially acute and predominant in several special areas.

One major area of crystallization of social problems can be found in situations affected by those roles formed with respect to individuals' primordial qualities, crystallized into special roles. These are, first, those involved with the life cycle of the individual in his transition through different age-stages; second, those involved with the definition of the sexual roles; and last, the combination of these two in the field of family and kinship.

These areas involve certain directly observable and experienceable biological properties—sexuality, position in the life cycle, genetic related-ness—and as such they are somewhat refractory vis-à-vis any institutional arrangement or cultural norm or definition. This vitality and autonomy becomes necessarily acute and articulated in times of social and cultural change, when existing, traditional norms which relate them to institu-tional frameworks are shattered.

Processes of modernization also generate problems with respect to community organization and organization of work and of leisure time activities. Just as in the cases of youth, age, and sexual and family relationships, these areas may escape full institutionalization and may provide points of recurrent eruptions of new social problems even after relatively successful attempts to solve the problems at one level of their development.

Social problems may also arise out of the fact that the institutional structure may not enable some of its members to perform the roles expected of them. In modern societies, beyond outright denial of rights, of discrimination, the area in which the access to the performance of roles may be denied to an individual through forces engendered by the institutional structure has been the most prevalent one—has been the area of work, which became, as we have seen earlier, dissociated from community and family spheres.

In the early stages of modernization and industrialization the problem of unemployment was perhaps the most acute problem. With the growth and stabilization of industrial society, this problem has taken on an additional dimension. In many cases unemployment caused by technical innovation continues to be very important. But in other parts of the technologically more advanced societies, there tend also to develop new social problems in the area of "leisure." Leisure as a specific problem seems also to arise under conditions of growing distinction between the sphere of work and that of nonwork. Just as the work situation became dissociated from more encompassing kinship and community relations, leisure time activities became dissociated from traditional play or ritual-situation, or even to some extent from spontaneous types of recreation within relatively fixed frameworks (as shown in the classical studies of Greece by Jane Harrison and Huizinga's analysis of the play element in modern culture [4]). It gradually became crystallized into a full-fledged problem area of its own, defined in its own terms and looking, as it were, for more encompassing forms of organization.

One of the latest manifestations of the conjunction between age and leisure problems has been the problem of people retired from full formal work activities who at the same time can no longer find any appreciable roles to perform within their families or communities.[5]

The concrete manifestations of social problems are varied, though often overlapping. One such manifestation has been the individual's withdrawal from undertaking and performance of major social roles— as manifested in suicide, vagrancy, and various types of illness and mental illness.[6] The more outright forms of deviance and norm-breaking were manifest mostly in various types of criminal activity.

Beyond these more specific behavioral manifestations the various social problems could also become manifest in more general feelings of dissatisfaction, of uneasiness, of feelings of anomie and powerlessness, of alienation of the individual or group from a broader community or from the larger society, from the political order and from the rulers who, even more than traditional rulers, believed that such a moral order should exist as a result of an all-encompassing ideology.

Around these ruptures in consensus and integration, certain types of dissensual formations group, ranging from the more ephemeral types of panic, mob outburst, etc., up to different types of more fully crystallized and continual subculture and anticulture.

It has been particularly around roles in the economy and in roles defined by the primordial qualities of sex and age that a dissensual integration has emerged. Movements have attempted to modify those aspects of the larger society which bear particularly on the roles in question. The working class and socialist movement on one side, and the movement for the rights of women and children and youth on the other, have been two major reactions to the process of modernization— they are, indeed, the features of any society at a certain stage of modernization.[7]

---

[4] J. Harrison, *Ancient Art and Ritual* (London: Oxford University Press, 1925); and J. Huizinga, *Homo Ludens: A Study of the Play Element in Culture* (London: Routledge & Kegan Paul, Ltd., 1949).

[5] Eisenstadt, ed., *op. cit.*

[6] *Ibid.*

[7] *Ibid.*

Beyond these there developed in all modern societies movements of protest and transformation around the central collectivity, around the definition of the collectivity; of which the various national movements (especially those with more populist orientations) are, of course, the most important here.[8]

As there are but few reliable data on these problems in premodern societies, it is of course difficult to know to what extent these various social problems developed in modern society more than in other types of societies, but several characteristics seem to stand out. One is that, on the whole, in modern societies these problems became related to some of the characteristics of the central spheres of society, to the growing participation of wider groups in the center of society, to the growing demands for civility and to a much lesser extent to "accidental" personal or family reasons. Second, in modern societies many of the traditional mechanisms of social control which dealt with these problems seem to have become much less effective. Thus the more informal type of social control, such as the pressures of kin and local groups or of local religious or secular leaders, became relatively ineffective in the more differentiated and changing circumstances attendant on the processes of modernization, while the new moral order of civility demanded much greater degree of self-control by individuals.

Thirdly, there can be no doubt that the public awareness of these problems and sensitivity to them became greater—mainly because of the weakening of the self-sufficiency of local units and the continual drawing in of various groups into the center of the society, the spread of the demands for greater participation in the central spheres of the society, and the stronger emphasis on the dignity of the individual.

SOCIAL PROBLEMS AND SOCIAL POLICY

Corresponding roughly to the "movements" of those affected by modernization processes have been the social policies undertaken by governments to cope with these same problems—from intentions not always identical with those of the movements. In governmental social policies the concern was with justice, but also with the maintenance of order while making concessions to the demands of the movements, and the conceptions of those outside them but sympathetic to them. In the movements there was also concern with justice, but more radically interpreted, without a commitment to the sacredness of the existing order.

The problems of unemployment and of conditions of work became objects of regulation by various "factory laws," and by various schemes of social security of legislation and of regularized, mutual bargaining be-

[8] E. Kadourie, *Nationalism* (London: Hutchinson & Co. (Publishers), Ltd., 1961).

tween employees and labor.[9] Similarly, education problems also became focuses of political bargaining on the one hand, and on the other hand objects of public policy dealing with establishment of compulsory education, and of regulating the differential access to education and the rights of private bodies to provide it.[10]

Modern municipal government, town planning, and housing schemes stepped in to deal with at least some of the problems of urban cooperation stemming from continual urbanization. Modern police forces were established to deal with delinquency and crime. Later various remedial measures developed, which often changed the structure of penal institutions of many countries. Moreover, new types of large-scale, professional organizations developed within all modern societies to deal with these problems.

And yet, while the development of such policies did very often solve the particular manifestation of the problems to which it was addressed, it was but rarely that any such concrete policy could solve, for a long period of time, all the possible or potential types of problems arising within any such major social sphere.

Thus new problems of adjustment to work and of unemployment developed with the continued spread of industrialization and with continual changes and advances in industrial techniques. For instance, social policies designed to deal with problems of elderly people in situations of poverty became relatively ineffectual in situations of relative affluence, where it was not lack of minimal financial support but rather the loss of jobs and meaningful social relations that became important.

THE CHANGING PATTERN OF YOUTH PROBLEMS

Out of such varied problems we shall concentrate here on the "youth problem" in its varied transformations as a good illustration of the persistence and transformation of some at least of the areas of social problems.[11]

The central concrete manifestations of youth problems in the first stages of modernization were two. The first one was of what may be called "social problems" of youth, developing out of urbanization, early industrialization, immigration, and the different problems of dislocation. The urban slum, the "street corner society," the "gang," have become the main symbols of this type of youth problem.

[9] H. L. Wilensky and C. N. Lebeaux, "Conceptions of Social Welfare," in Eisenstatdt, ed., *op. cit.*, pp. 420-39.

[10] R. H. Titmuss, *Essays on the Welfare State* (London: George Allen & Unwin, 1958); and R. H. Titmuss, "The National Health Service in England," in Eisenstadt, ed., *op. cit.* 440-48.

[11] S. N. Eisenstadt, "Changing Pattern of Youth Problems in Contemporary Societies," *Essays in Comparative Institution* (New York: John Wiley & Sons, Inc., 1965).

The second major manifestation of youth problems in modern society was that of different youth movements, student movements, and spontaneous youth organizations which developed, beginning in central Europe in the early part of the nineteenth century, among university students strongly influenced by romanticism, with its emphasis on the unspoiled individuality of the youth taking part in wider social movements or aiming at the reformation of the society in terms of some distinct, specific youth values. This participation in the various movements was part of wider phenomena of dissatisfaction, of "restlessness" of youth in its confrontation with the cultural and political frameworks and symbols presented to it by the new patterns of society then developing.

It is in these movements that the social dynamics of modern youth has found its first fullest expression. It is in them that dreams of a new life, a new society, freedom and spontaneity, a new humanity and aspirations to social and cultural change, to new cultural symbols and symbols of collective identity, have found utterance.

These major initial types of youth groups and problems have also inevitably greatly influenced the attitudes of social policy with regard to the problems of youth. One such attitude was manifest in the attempts of all social movements and political parties to absorb the potential social political interest and wider orientations of the youth groups into their own frameworks. Special youth sections or organizations were developed by most political and social groups.

Similarly, there have developed many agencies of what has been called "civic education"—youth clubs, playgrounds, etc.—whose main aims were to channelize the potential civic orientations into accepted and "safe" channels and to show a "peaceful" way of absorbing into the more central institutions the less developed, more peripheral groups of the society, which yet constituted the majority of the population.

These activities have very often overlapped, but certainly were not identical with the second more specific type of social policies which were developed to deal with youth problems, especially problems related to occupational and educational guidance. A major aim of these policies was to deal with a general amelioration of external conditions of life in urban centers and to provide youth with many amenities and services that they lacked in the new urban environments.

Third were the various corrective systems, ranging from probation officers and juvenile judges to social work agencies that strived to establish adequate means of control of the more disruptive aspects or manifestations of youth.

Since World War II, and especially in the Fifties, the forms of youth rebellion and youth problems have changed greatly and become diversified. Side by side with the older types of youth problems, which will presumably continue to persist, many new ones have developed, and the older have taken on new forms. Thus, politically oriented youth and students can be found in some countries—especially in Latin America in the so-called political university—in a somewhat new type or form of youth or student rebellion. Similarly, in Japan there developed among the students some intensive political activities, best exemplified by the Zengakuren which, while having many traits in common with the older type of student unrest, are yet much more active and "anarchist" than most.[12] In many countries, such as India,[13] student unrest does not necessarily take on the form of express political activities; it is very often focused more against authority in general, as manifest in the university. Similarly, the problem of dislocation, of delinquency stemming out of rapid urbanization and migration, has also been found both in many countries or sectors in the first stages of industrialization or of excessive urbanization. But side by side with these more "traditional" types of youth, new types of youth culture and problems developed. Developments have, on the whole, changed and diversified the overall picture of youth problems and youth rebellions.

These various new types of youth culture evince several common characteristics. One of these is that the span of areas of social life that the specific youth culture encompasses tends to expand constantly. First, it extends over a longer period of life. Second, it extends now to include areas of work, of leisure time activity, and of many interpersonal relations. Third, the potential and actual autonomy of these groups and their direct access to various spheres of adult society—to the sphere of work, of marriage and family life, of political participation, of consumption— have greatly increased and their dependence on adults has greatly decreased.

But, paradoxically enough, this growing direct access of young people to the various areas of life gives rise to a growing insecurity of status—of occupational and economic status, of communal participation, of status in the family—and to a feeling of alienation from processes of historical change.

Perhaps the most widely noticed type of such rebellions has been that of the "Teddy Boys," the insecure offenders, the "Halbstarke." [14] In a way, these new developments have called for much attention and have also given rise to most of the new pedagogical literature dealing with these problems. But even this phenomenon, which has been very often treated as a relatively homogeneous and unified one, is really greatly differentiated. Its different manifestations differ to some extent according

[12] R. J. Lifton, "Youth and History: Individual Change in Post-war Japan," *Daedalus*, **91**, 1 (Winter 1962), 172-97.
[13] M. Weiner, *The Politics of Scarcity: Public Pressure and Political Response in India* (Chicago: University of Chicago Press, 1962), Chap. 7.
[14] T. R. Fyvel, *The Insecure Offenders* (London: Penguin Books, Ltd., 1963).

to class and occupational origins and backgrounds, according to age and marital status of parents, according to educational experience, as well as according to the prevailing "cultural" and political atmosphere.

These characteristics have been manifest in the marked change in the character and scale of juvenile delinquency in many countries—a continual increase in the more "violent" types of delinquent activities as against the more "traditional" trends of petty crimes.

While these characteristics have found their most extreme manifestations in various types of delinquency and in extreme literary movements, they have also appeared in varying degrees in most other types of youth culture. They were manifest in the social and cultural participation that began to be characterized by a growing shift to more individualistic, "hedonist" values, to weakening of orientations, to collective goals—although very often there were also many new "positive" potential developments in the form of new possibilities and avenues for creative individual and group activity.

The most important new factor affecting the problem of youth was the growth of occupational specialization and of economic planning, and the growth of bureaucratization of most types of economic markets, as well as increase in the close interrelationship between occupational placement and educational attainments.

The continual expansion of educational facilities and of market economy with its growing pressures for different types of occupational systems has, in general, greatly increased the direct connections between educational attainment and economic opportunities and occupational placement. This has created greater possibilities of vocational guidance, but has also given rise to new problems.

The growing economic specialization had the double effect of increasing the demand for special skills and creating difficulties for those with only more "general" preparation or education; an education geared neither to some "traditional" occupations, to any declining crafts, nor to the expanding industrial labor force market.

One such major problem was the different types of "drop-outs." [15] This problem of drop-outs has not been confined to the older types of professional, "intellectual," or student unemployment, but became extended even to the lower echelons of the primary school levels, which have become especially important both in many of the newly developing societies and in the many "underdeveloped pockets" of highly industrialized societies.

A closely related series of problems arose in this connection through the varied systems of educational selection, which have become fully or partially institutionalized in many modern societies, the most extreme

[15] T. Hus'en, "Educational Structure and the Development of Ability," in A. Halsey, *Ability and Educational Opportunity* (Paris, 1961), pp. 113-34.

examples of which can be found in England and in Sweden, but which can be found in some form in almost all other modern countries.[16] Within this range, the most important series of problems was that related to the early entry into an educational course which fixes the range of occupations into which the young person can enter, thereby restricting later mobility and giving rise to a feeling of being constricted within a relatively expanding society and economy.

The various changes in youth culture described above were also greatly influenced by developments in the sphere of values and of culture. Perhaps the most important single overall development in this field has been the transfer of emphasis from the creation and participation in the forging of future-oriented collective values, to the growing institutionalization of such values, whether in a coercive, dissensual, or consensual manner. In a great variety of ways, these have been common to many different countries.

In Russia, youth movements became officially, coercively institutionalized through the organization of the Komsomol. In many European countries the institutionalizing of youth groups, agencies, and ideologies came through association with political parties, or through acceptance as part of the educational system—an acceptance that sometimes entailed supervision by the public or governmental authorities. In the United States, many (such as the Boy Scouts) have become an accepted part of community life and, to some extent, a symbol of differential social status. In many Asian and African countries, organized youth movements have become part of the nationalistic movements and, the nation's independence won, part of the official educational organizations.

From the point of view of their impact on youth these processes have had several important results. The possibility of linking personal transition both to social groups and to cultural values—so strongly emphasized in the youth movements and noticeable to some extent even in the looser youth culture—has been greatly weakened. The social and sometimes even the cultural dimension of the future may thus be flattened and emptied. The various collective values become transformed. Instead of being remote goals resplendent with romantic dreams, they have become mundane objectives of the present, with its shabby details of daily politics and administration. More often than not they are intimately connected with the processes of bureaucratization.

Thus youth in many such countries, be they new states, communist states, or European welfare states, face not only "reactionary" parents who do not want to allow them to change society, but also successful revolutionaries, people whose revolutions have succeeded and through

[16] R. Ulich, ed., *The Education of Nations* (Cambridge, Mass.: Harvard University Press, 1961); and A. Kerr, *The Schools of Europe* (Westminster, Md.: Canterbury Press, 1962), esp. Chaps. 5, 6.

this success have become part of a new "establishment," creating a new collective reality.

All these developments have greatly changed the attitudes of youth to the common symbols of the community, their perception of their own participation in the framework of such a community, and the relations between generations in a way that has not been known before. From the point of view of our analysis they provide one of the most interesting illustrations of the perenniality—and transformation—of so-called social problems in modern societies.

STRUCTURAL CHANGE AND ORIENTATIONS OF PROTEST

However important the various social problems were, and however much they became focuses of social policy only under very specific conditions, they did touch directly on the central institution and cultural society, and thereby became focuses and symbols of political disputes. In several concrete cases, as for instance when some of these problems and their symbols became focuses of some of the movements discussed above, social problems may have become of central symbolic importance.

By their very nature the various social problems were more related to various processes of social disorganization, and not to the overall changes in the internal social structure of the major groups and in their place in the society. It was out of these changes that the major movements and orientations of protest and transformation within the central, cultural, and political spheres of modern societies developed.

Needless to say, movements of protest and transformation, in the cultural and political spheres, tend to develop in all societies in a great variety of forms, be they rebellions or sectarian uprisings, and often to precipitate the downfall of states or churches. But in most premodern societies the influence of these movements oscillated, as it were, between two extremes—between relative "a-politicization" and great isolation from the central political and cultural institutions on the one hand, and direct participation in the overthrowing of a given regime on the other.[17] Only rarely in premodern societies did such movements constitute a relatively orderly part of the central political process.

In modern societies, however, with the growing differentiation, structural specialization, and interdependence between different groups of the society; with the bringing together of various groups into a framework of common interaction; and with the growing impingement of various peripheral groups on the centers of the society, i.e., with the growth of trend to consensual mass society—the movements and orientations of protest became much more closely related to the central political processes.

[17] S. N. Eisenstadt, *The Political System of Empires* (New York: Free Press of Glencoe, Inc., 1963).

As a result of these tendencies there developed a growing interrelation between the various problems of major social groups and the central political process. These various problems, be they economic, social, religious, or cultural, could become focuses of two different and yet closely interrelated patterns of political demands and protest. On the one hand —often in close relation to the various problems stemming out of the various processes of disorganization analyzed above—they could easily become focuses of various concrete demands for special economic, political, or administrative privileges, or for taking care of their economic or organizational problems. On the other hand, they could also become focuses of broader, more general and symbolic demands for changes in some more central features of the social structure.

THE MAJOR THEMES OF SOCIAL PROTEST

It was out of these general structural transformations characteristic of modernization that the major orientations of protest in the political, social, and cultural sphere tended to develop. The common denominator of these orientations was, first, their aiming at transformation of the newly emerging social and political centers and their symbols and of broader social structure, and second, their relatively wide spread among the major articulate groups and strata of the society. Some of these themes of protest focused mainly on problems of social order, and some more on those of cultural tradition—but very often they were closely interrelated. The first basic theme was the search for principles of social order and justice, and of the legitimation of the center in general and the ruling groups in particular in terms of some nontraditional values, acceptable to broader strata and to some extent shared and even "created" by them. These could be some social values, i.e., values related to some of the problems of distributive justice referred to above, of the representation of the symbols of the overall collectivity, of efficiency, or of legality.[18] Here problems of allocations of different resources—power, wealth, status—and of access to various positions within the society, to different groups and strata, were also central.[19]

The second theme focused on the nature of the new, emerging overall civil, political, and cultural community—especially on the search for new common symbols in which various groups of the society could find some sense of personal and collective identity.[20] The problem of the relevance

---

[18] On the variety of modern social and especially socialist thought see, for instance, A. Fried and R. Sanders, eds., *Socialist Thought* (New York: Doubleday Anchor Books, 1964).

[19] On the variety of modern political thought, especially as related to problems of legitimation, etc., see, for instance, W. Ebenstein, ed., *Man and the State: Modern Political Ideas* (New York: Holt, Rinehart & Winston, Inc., 1947).

[20] *Ibid.*, Chap. 14.

of the tradition and history of the community to the problems attendant
on modernization and to the new institutional setting first became a very
important focus of debate. Second, and closely connected to the first, was
the search for some symbols and roles that would combine both general
universal orientations, inherent as these were in basic cultural orientations
of modernity, with the particular national traditions, and to find within
these last the bases for maintenance of a civil order.[21]

The third major theme of protest was focused around the possibility
of attaining full expression of human and cultural creativity, of personal
dignity and of true or pure interpersonal relation, within the specialized
and differentiated frameworks attendant on modernization and the complex division of labor involved.[22] Basic to this theme was the problem
of so-called "alienation," i.e., of the assumed loss by individuals of direct
relation to and identification with their work, their social setting, and
other people.[23]

Around all these focal themes of protest there could develop different
basic views or orientations, which often tended to overlap. One such orientation, usually called the "rightist" one, was rooted in the constant feeling,
by groups attached to what they regarded as the previously prevailing
order, of being ousted from existing positions and values, of losing their
place in the society; and the consequent development by them of demands
for upholding and/or restoration of traditional order and values.[24] The
second extreme, which may be called the "leftist" orientation, was geared
to effecting far-reaching change in the social structure, in the basic principles of allocation in favor of groups or classes which allegedly were
deprived of advantageous position or of full participation. These groups
could be social classes, occupational categories, regional groups within
any certain society, or special overall national or tribal subgroups within
a broad or international social and political order.[25]

Both these orientations could become interrelated in different ways with
the search for direct, "pure," unalienated human relations and attach-
ments to primordial symbols. Traditionalists would claim that such relations are possible only under relatively stable, ordered conditions,
undiluted by the disrupting forces of growing differentiation, democratization, and mass society. Political "radicals," on the other hand, could claim
that such relation could be achieved only by overthrowing such order and
establishing a new one whose institutional arrangements will entirely

[21] E. Shils, "Tradition and Liberty: Antinomy and Interdependence," *Ethics,* 68,
3 (April 1958), 153-65.
[22] A. Fried, R. Sanders, and M. Buber, eds., *Paths in Utopia* (New York: The
Macmillan Company, 1950), Chaps. 3, 7.
[23] T. B. Bottomore and M. Rubel, eds., *Karl Marx: Selected Writings in Sociology
and Social Philosophy* (London: C. A. Watts and Co., Ltd., 1961), pp. 167-77.
[24] See Ebenstein, *op. cit.,* Chaps. 5, 6, 7, 8.
[25] See Fried and Sanders, eds., *op. cit.*

coalesce with "nonalienated" relations. Other, more "nonpolitical" radicals could claim that such relations could be attained only outside of both traditional and any modern, formalized power-order.

THE MAJOR THEMES OF CULTURAL PROTEST

Such orientations of protest, aiming at the transformation of the major symbols of community, developed also in the cultural sphere proper.

The major themes that developed in this sphere throughout different stages of modernization were those of traditionalism as against more autonomous forces of cultural creativity, and of the relation of both of these to the possibility of erosion of cultural creativity and standards.[26]

The first specific form of cleavage or of problems that developed in this sphere was that of religious freedom and of the possibility of an overall secularization of culture. But the general problems persisted in various forms beyond this specific first cleavage.

Around these problems there also developed relatively distinctive types of overall orientations and attitudes, not dissimilar from those in the socio-political sphere proper. The traditionalist, the extreme antitraditionalist, and those orientations which tended to stress more the possibility of autonomous developments in the field of culture and sciences faced one another very often.

One tendency was that of the elitist protest against the supposed erosion of cultural traditions and standards, and the attempt to uphold various types of traditional and "close" elitist values and circles as against the encroachments of unprincipled eroding developments of the "mass" consumption of culture.[27]

These elitist orientations could develop in two different directions: the purely traditionalist-conservative or fundamentalist way, or through the search for some new elite groups in which nontraditional cultural orientation could be upheld as against the more eroding mechanical tendency of mass culture. The other extreme type of cultural orientation has been the populist one, characterized by an attitude emphasizing the almost total identity and predominance of the popular forms and levels of culture in the sphere of cultural creativity, of the identity between the cultural center and the periphery. Such populist tendencies could take on a variety of concrete forms and could, paradoxically, become closely assimilated into "conservative" and radical orientations and movements.[28]

These varied elitist, nonelitist, and populist orientations could, to some

[26] E. Shils, "Mass Society and Its Culture," *Diogenes,* **29** (Spring 1960), 288-314.
[27] D. Bell, "Modernity and Mass Society: On the Varieties of Cultural Experience," *Studies in Public Communication,* **4** (1962), 3-34.
[28] E. Shils, *The Torment of Secrecy* (New York: Free Press of Glencoe, Inc., 1956), *passim.*

extent at least, cut across all political camps. Both the "leftist" and the "rightist" groups and orientations there tended to develop both "elitist" and "populist" or "mass" orientations and organizations.

These basic socio-political and cultural orientations could be found in different varieties and constellations in all modern societies and in different social and political camps and they tended, of course, to coalesce in varying ways, although each of these orientations of protest or of demands for the reshaping and recrystallization of the political, social, and cultural order tended to develop, to some extent at least, according to its own dynamics.

The concrete issues and problems around which these broader "protest" orientations could become focused have necessarily changed throughout the different periods of modernization, at different stages of modernization and in various different societies and settings—but in one way or another they persisted throughout all the different processes of modernization.

INTERNATIONAL ASPECTS OF PROTEST

These social and cultural orientations and symbols of social justice and tradition, and the various attempts to define the overall cultural and political community in terms of these values and symbols, developed not only *within* each national community, but also very largely with respect to the international sphere.

First, as we have already shown above, many of the modern social movements—such as socialist, communist, or national movements—were international in scope and orientation. Second, with the growing interrelations and interdependence between nations and with the unification of the international scene, international relations also became conceived more and more in terms of distributive justice.

This perhaps had its roots in the nature of the encounter between the latecomers to modernization and the first-comers (especially England and France) in general and between the Asian and African nations and the Europeans in particular, and in the colonial situation that has developed as one of the main patterns of interrelations between them. Hence the self-perception of many New Nations—to use Lipset's expression, beginning with "the first New Nation—the U.S." [29] in terms of social justice and cultural attainments, was not only or even mainly directed inwardly, but was also conceived in terms of their interrelation to other nations and their international standing.

[29] S. M. Lipset, *The First New Nation* (New York: Basic Books, Inc., Publishers, 1961).

The preceding analysis indicates that the
various tendencies of disorganization of
social groups and the various types
of "protest" orientations and demands are,
in a sense, inherent in the processes of
modernization and constitute basic
features of modern societies.

These protests and demands manifest
themselves, in modern societies, in two
closely interwoven ways. One is the search
for ways of regulating the varied, discrete,
and often conflicting interests of different
groups. The other is that of search for,
and attempts to crystallize, new major
symbols of personal and collective
(usually national) identity.

But perhaps even more significant than
each of these types of problem was the fact
of growing interconnection between them.
The various discrete and concrete interests
of various groups, be they economic,
religious, or political problems, tended
more and more—although in different
degrees in different places—to be perceived
and defined not only in terms of their
immediate, concrete settings but also in
broader terms; of social justice, of
participation in the broader collectivity, of
the primordial images
of this collectivity.

This connection between demands related
to concrete problems and those connected

CHAPTER THREE   to the general principles of justice and to

Structural Change, Structural Diversity, and Problems of Sustained Growth in Modernization

the primordial collective qualities is rooted in the basic characteristics of modern societies—in the continual growing differentiation, in the bringing together of differentiated groups into common frameworks which increased their interdependence on all levels of social life, and in the growing impingement of these groups on the center of the society; i.e., in the mass-consensual characteristics of modern societies.

These characteristics of modern societies explain why orientations and demands of protest and transformation constitute a part of the wider process through which various groups and strata attempt to articulate their problems, in the more differentiated social structure and in its central spheres.

Many of the objects of protest and demands constituted some of the major focuses of political struggle, and were, as we have seen, objects of social policies developed by the ruling elites of these societies. Among these we may mention such problems as agrarian reform; labor relations and organization; the regulation and control of different types of markets (goods, labor, money, and credit) in the economic field; problems of development and integration of the national community and of the crystallization of its identity, of its relation to different parts of its historical tradition, in the political spheres; problems of relations between the educational system and social and occupational mobility; and the extent of autonomy of professional organization in the broader social field.

This means, as has already been indicated, that the orientations of protest and the movements of demand related to them have to be seen as more extreme manifestations of the regular workings of the political institutions, and must therefore be analyzed within this context.

These various demands were articulated and aggregated in the major types of political organizations prominent in modern societies analyzed above—in interest groups, movements, public opinion, and political parties.

The interest groups tended to emphasize the more restricted, discrete interests of different groups, and "restricted" social movements and "public opinion" tended to emphasize demands for the reformation of existing political institutions, while the more extreme social movements emphasized demands for total transformation of political regimes. Different party or partylike organs may of course evince different degrees of predominance of each of these types of organizations and of their respective political orientations. But whatever such relative predominance, the integration of each of these elements into the frameworks of parties is never complete, and interest groups, social movements, and different organs of public opinion tend to develop autonomous orientations, and in many situations tend to burst the frameworks imposed on them by the parties. They tend to maintain their autonomous orientations through the presentation of their own demands directly to the central political institutions—executive, legislative, or bureaucratic—without the mediation of any given party, through attempts to mobilize support and resources for themselves directly rather than through a party, as well as attempts to interpret different political demands within their own frameworks.

Hence also the possibility of the persistence and transformation of protest in its different manifestations has been inherent in modern institutional settings, no matter how well organized they might have become. It was chiefly these autonomous expressions of interest groups, public opinion, and social movements that constituted the major focuses of perspective of social protest in the political field.[1]

DEVELOPMENT OF CHANGE-ABSORBING INSTITUTIONS

Whatever the differences between the scope and intensity of protest demands in various modern societies, a very crucial common characteristic of them all can be discerned, namely the fact that they all not only have to cope with certain relatively fixed sets of problems, but face continually new and changing problems. Indeed, all the major types of institutional and political mechanisms outlined above are to at least some extent attuned to this possibility.

In most modern societies there developed, in conjunction with the processes of structural differentiation and of the impingement of the wider groups on the center, some ways and mechanisms to deal with such continually changing problems, and with the complex problems of coordination, regulation, and integration. These regulative mechanisms are of two basic kinds. One is the establishment of certain relatively efficient institutional frameworks, as well as organizations capable of regulating them and providing adequate administrative services and injunctions for regulating the growing conflicts between various groups. The other is the development of values and symbols acceptable to large parts of the population that upheld the various regulations and injunctions developed within these institutional frameworks. These two aspects of regulative mechanisms are to a large extent parallel to Durkheim's distinction between the contractual and the precontractual elements in social organization,[2] and the extent to which they tend to develop together constitutes a crucial problem facing all modernizing and modern societies.

The most important means for the development of such institutional mechanisms has been the development of various *generalized* media of exchange that are not embedded in any ascriptive unit and can assure the

[1] S. N. Eisenstadt, "Political Modernization: Some Comparative Notes," *International Journal of Comparative Sociology*, 5, 1 (March 1964), 3-24; and W. Kornhauser, *The Politics of Mass Society* (New York: Free Press of Glencoe, Inc., 1959).

[2] E. Durkheim, *The Division of Labour in Society* (New York: Free Press of Glencoe, Inc., 1947); and K. Mannheim, *Freedom, Power and Democratic Planning* (New York: Oxford University Press, Inc., 1950).

flow of resources between different societal units.[3] Money and monetary credit is perhaps the best example of such generalized media. Similar, if less generalized, arrangements for the flow of generalized political support through voting parties also developed in other institutional fields. These media of exchange constituted the *means* for effective regulation of the relations between different groups in the society, and the assurance of their regular flow within any society facilitated the development of the regulative integrative mechanisms.

Among such various integrative mechanisms—which although existing to some degree in premodern societies, became more fully institutionalized in modern ones—we may mention first the development of law and complex and autonomous legal systems, especially of civil law and of law of contracts, as relatively independent of political authority.[4] Second are various large-scale coordinating agencies; especially various bureaucratic organizations which developed in all social spheres, be they economic, political, or cultural.[5] Third are various associational and professional organizations, and fourth, various markets and market mechanisms that regulate the flow of resources in different spheres according to the laws of demand and supply. Last, and perhaps most important from the point of view of our analysis, are various political organizations and some of the specific aspects of political process, with their emphasis on legislation as an instrument of conscious change, with the interplay between different types of political organizations, and the possibility of their integration, through party or partylike activities in a relatively orderly way, into the central political institutions.

Similarly, the various provisions for orderly change of rulers as embodied in the system of election of constitutional or multi-party regimes are perhaps the most important examples of such institutional mechanisms oriented to absorption of change. From this point of view it is significant that some symbolic elections are also held in nondemocratic regimes (especially totalitarian, but also in most modern autocratic regimes), and that these symbolic elections are viewed as providing at least some of the legislation of the regime.

The proliferation of different governmental agencies, as well as the formal differentiation between them, also enables the continual functioning of some services and political activities, irrespective of the daily vicissitudes of political struggle. It also facilitates the development of a

[3] T. Parsons, *Structure and Process in Modern Societies* (New York: Free Press of Glencoe, Inc., 1959).

[4] M. Rheinstein, ed., *Max Weber on Law in Economy and Society,* trans. E. Shils (Cambridge, Mass.: Harvard University Press, 1954); and *ibid.*

[5] M. Weber, *The Theory of Social and Economic Organization,* trans. T. Parsons and A. M. Henderson (New York: Oxford University Press, Inc., 1947), 329-40; and H. Gerth and C. W. Mills, eds., *From Max Weber* (London: Routledge and Kegan Paul, Ltd., 1947), pp. 196-244.

more dispersed consensus, extended to different aspects of political life and institutions.

And yet, although institutional frameworks with some ability to absorb changes tend to develop to some extent in most modern societies, their mere development does not assure the adequate and continuous absorption, within the modern institutional structure, of continually changing problems, and the capacity to deal with such changes effectively varies greatly between different modern societies.

These institutional arrangements serve as mechanisms through which the various contractual arrangements are regulated and upheld. But in order to be effective in the long run they have also to be upheld by pre-contractual symbols and orientations. The extent to which such symbols and orientations and the appropriate institutional frameworks develop is not assured by the development of these varied institutional arrangements outlined above; the two may develop in different degrees.

The history of modern social systems is full of cases of unsuccessful adaptation, or of lack of adaptation of existing structures to new types of problems and organizations and of the lack of ability of these institutions to assimilate, to some extent, the various movements of protest inherent in the process of modernization.[6]

The external manifestations of such blocking are usually some types of political "eruptions," i.e., of more or less violent outbreaks of political activities and development of symbols oriented against the existing system and its symbols. The strength of such eruptions, as well as their repercussions on the stability of the regimes in which they take place, varies greatly from place to place. But the possibility of eruptions, of lack of absorption of change, is as inherent in the processes of modernization and the structure of modern society as are the tendencies to continual change.

Such eruptions may lead either to the transformation of the existing regime into a more flexible one, better adapted to deal with continually changing problems, or to breakdowns of modernization, to the development of regressive or deformed regimes with autocratic tendencies, as in the case of Fascism and Nazism; to outright attempts at deformation of modernity and of civil society and to outright demodernization.[7]

SYSTEM TRANSFORMATION AND SUSTAINED GROWTH

All the varied characteristics of modern societies outlined above, their mass-consensual orientation, their continual structural differentiation and impingement of broader groups on the center of the society, indicate what

---

[6] S. N. Eisenstadt, "Breakdowns of Modernization," *Economic Development and Cultural Change*, 12, 4 (July 1964), 345-67.

[7] *Ibid.*

probably is the most central problem of modernization—its inherent tendency to system transformation.

The nature of this tendency can be brought out by the two following quotations from recent works. M. Halpern defines it as follows:

. . . the revolution of modernization involves transformation—the transformation of all systems by which man organizes his society, that is, his political, social, economic, intellectual, religious, and psychological systems . . .

. . . The revolution of modernization is the first revolution of mankind to set a new price upon stability in any system of society—namely, it requires an enduring capacity to generate and absorb persistent transformation. This capacity represents at the same the time the minimum and maximum requirements for wedding stability and change once crucial elements and linkages of a traditional system cease to function. To maintain such a capacity for transformation constitutes both the uniquely modern opportunity—which many elites do not yet recognize or desire—and the uniquely modern requirement —which many elites may fail to meet—for succeeding in the fundamental revolution of our times. Traditional societies, by contrast, were not faced continuously by system-transforming demands. When, usually only after centuries, they were confronted by a particular challenge of this kind, they were capable of responding only by disintegrating or by creating a new closed system.

Modernization demands of all systems of society the capacity which the scientific community already possesses: the ability to persist continuously in the enterprise of responding to the challenge of new questions, new facts, and inadequate solutions by developing, maintaining, modifying, and disintegrating systems of theory. That such scientific revolutions, even under the best of circumstances, tend to be discontinuous, conflict-ridden, and marked by considerable intervals of concentration on refining and enlarging existing systems, helps to make scientific revolutions particularly characteristic examples of the revolution of modernization.[8]

Edward Shils' definition of modernity, especially as it is perceived nowadays in the New States, brings out these characteristics in an even sharper way:

Among the elites of the New States, "modern" means dynamic, concerned with people, democratic and equalitarian, scientific, economically advanced, sovereign and influential.

Modern states must be "dynamic" above all else. To be modern, an elite, as the elites of the New States see it, must not fear change; on the contrary, it must strive to bring it about. It does not wish to remain as it is. It is against the ancient regime, even where it affirms the past of the country, it stresses its adaptability to the needs of the present. "Dynamic" is one of the favorite adjectives of the elites of the New States. The elites pride themselves on their dynamism and they claim that the mass of the population demands it of

[8] M. Halpern, "The Rate and Costs of Political Development," *Annals of the American Academy of Political and Social Science,* **358** (March 1965), 21-23.

them. Almost everything else which they esteem presupposes this praise of change.[9]

The root of this basic tendency to change, to improvement, to continuous system transformation, lies in the very nature of modernity, not only as a structural characteristic of a society, but also as a cultural ideal or value, as a more or less conscious goal of elites and broader groups alike. It is this which distinguishes between modern and other social systems. All societies, from the primitive up to the great historical empires, have been undergoing processes of change, and in many of them, as for instance in the empires, many such processes of change were initiated consciously by the rulers or by various political or religious elites.[10] And yet, in certain crucial aspects these processes of change differed not only quantitatively but also qualitatively from those of modern societies.

However much various elites of these empires promoted political, social, or cultural change, these changes were envisaged as part of a given order—which these rulers or elites interpret or represent in a better way than other groups, but which in itself was traditionally given, was not change-oriented, and was oriented more to the maintenance of a cosmic, trans-societal rather than of a social order.[11] Moreover, the interpretation of such tradition was exclusively in the hands of such elites, and it was they who monopolized the political and cultural centers of these societies. The broader strata could identify themselves with this center and the order represented by it. They were, in fact, expected to do so, but in themselves could not participate in the formulation of its major symbols or organizations and in the active interpretation of these traditions.

The great breakthrough to modernity has been both in the great change in the contents of the symbols of the center, in their secularization, and in the growing emphasis on values of human dignity and social equality as well; and in the growing possibility of the participation, even if in an intermittent or partial way, of broader groups in the formulations of its central symbols and institutions. This breakthrough contains within itself the specific characteristics of social changes in modernity, the propensity to system transformation and the persistence of demands for change, protest, and transformation. These demands to change could, of course, develop in different directions; they could be reformatory, demanding the improvement of existing institutions, or they could aim at total transformation of a system. But in one way or another they constituted basic characteristics of all modern societies.

[9] E. Shils, *Political Development in the New States* (New York: Humanities Press, 1964), pp. 7-8.

[10] S. N. Eisenstadt, *The Political Systems of Empires* (New York: Free Press of Glencoe, Inc., 1963).

[11] *Ibid.*

Modernization evinces thus two closely connected but distinct aspects. The first is the development of a social structure with great variety of structural differentiation and diversification, of continually changing structural forms, activities, and problems, and of propensities to continual change and system transformation. But the mere development of these propensities does not in itself assume the development of an institutional structure capable of dealing in a relatively stable way with these continual changes and concomitantly of assuring the maintenance of a civil order. Thus the crucial problem that modernization creates in its wake is that of the ability of the emerging social structure to deal with such continual changes, or in other words, the problem of *sustained* development, i.e., the ability of developing an institutional structure capable of absorbing continually changing problems and demands.[12] It is this which constitutes the central problem and challenge of modernization.

STRUCTURAL DIVERSITY

Hitherto we have emphasized the common characteristics and problems of modernization. However, beyond these common features many differences developed in various modern and modernizing societies—differences in the structural characteristics of modernization, in the concrete constellations of the problems attendant on the development of modernization, and in the ways in which these problems were dealt with.

Such structural variety is discernible even at a first glimpse at the wide panorama of different modern or modernizing societies.[13] Thus, taking the relatively simple index of social mobilization, or of the extent of social differentiation, we see that the various modern societies, at what may seem to be similar stages of development, may differ greatly with regard to the extent of urbanization of literacy or of exposure to mass media.

Great differences may also be found between different modern societies in their major structural characteristics—in the extent of differentiation of roles and collectivities between and within the different institutional spheres, and in the nature and scope of the new, more specialized collectivities that tend to develop within each institutional sphere.

The extent of differentiation of roles and collectivities can vary not only between different societies but also between different institutional spheres of the same society. Thus in some societies, especially in the new states, we find, as we shall see in greater detail later, a greater extent of differentiation in the political sphere where universal political rights, political parties, and central administration develop, than in the

---

[12] Shils, *op. cit.*; and Halpern, *op. cit.*

[13] S. N. Eisenstadt, *Modernization, Growth and Diversity,* Carnegie faculty seminar (Bloomington, Ind.: Department of Government, Indiana University, 1963).

economic sphere, which is still largely traditional; while in other states, as for instance in many autocratic regimes of Latin America, Spain, or eastern Europe between the two world wars, the situation may have been reversed. Similarly, modern societies could differ with regard to the structure of the major collectivities and the relative importance of different institutional spheres.

Thus almost all societies in which modernization came relatively late —e.g., eastern European, Middle Eastern, and later also Asian societies— have evinced a greater predilection to the development of state control over most economic and educational organizations, of large-scale organizations with greater degree of merging of functions (i.e., political and economic) within them. Perhaps even more interesting is the case of Japan, where the process of modernization has not only retained many of the more traditional patterns of social life, or incorporated them into the developing modern frameworks, but the very process of modernization has been connected with the proliferation of new, continually expanding, relatively particularistic units such as the school clique, companies, and company unions which start to operate and coalesce after a relatively brief period in which universalistic and achievement criteria prevail.

Various modern societies may also differ with regard to the relative importance of the major mechanisms of allocation and regulation of social roles and activities, analyzed above. While the different types of allocative mechanisms exist in all modern societies, the extent of their relative predominance varies greatly between different societies.

Closely related to such relative predominance of different integrative mechanisms is the relative importance of the major political institutions —the executive, the legislative, the party, the bureaucratic, etc.—as the major focuses of political decision making and innovation; as well as the relative importance of each of the major forms of political expression and aggregation, i.e., interest groups, social movements, or public opinion.

Different modern societies differed also in some basic characteristics of their class structure. In some, like Europe, and to some extent also Middle Eastern and Latin American countries, strong landed aristocracies existed which dominated the upper echelons of the social structure, while in others, like India or Japan, no strong landed aristocracies were predominant for any long period. But even in Europe the aristocracies differed greatly according to the extent to which they were relatively independent of royal power or, conversely, were mainly service aristocracies.

Moreover, the composition of the middle classes, of the so-called bourgeoisie, differed greatly, even at similar levels of economic development. Thus, while in western Europe and to some extent in Latin

America the middle classes were initially composed of self-employed private merchants and industrialists and professionals, in Japan and in most of the new states the salaried bourgeoisie and professionals employed in large-scale bureaucratic enterprises were predominant. Great differences existed also with regard to the steepness of the social pyramids.

Modern or modernizing societies also differed greatly with regard to the extent to which they retained various elements of traditional social structure, attempted to obliterate them, or tended to develop within them various ways of revival of traditional forces. Even in most European countries we find a very great variety of ways of incorporation of traditional elements and orientations within the more differentiated modern frameworks, of ways in which ascriptive and particularistic criteria spread out and became crystallized within these frameworks, and of ways in which different functions coalesce within the same collectivities or organizations.

Most of these differences are not simply matters of stages of development—they do not denote stages which each modernizing and modern society has to go through in order to attain the capacity to system transformation.[14]

True, it is possible to talk about stages of modernization in terms of the degree of social mobilization and differentiation, and of some structural corollaries of such stages—for instance, the greater the scope of such mobilization the greater also will be the tendency to develop large-scale organizations. But most of the variations mentioned above or all the various combinations between them cannot be explained in terms of such stages.

As we shall see in greater detail later, many of them cut across such stages. Of special importance in this respect is the fact that different modern societies, which may on the whole belong to the same stage in terms of some general degree of social mobilization, do vary greatly with regard to the extent of such differentiation within the institutional sphere or in the center as contrasted with the periphery.

These differences are very often related to different temporal sequences of modernization in the major institutional spheres; to the fact that different modern or modernizing societies may go through such different temporal paths, thus emphasizing the fact that there exists no single road to modernity.

Certainly modernization creates everywhere some common problems, especially those rooted in the very process of differentiation, in mass-consensual tendencies and in the tendencies to system transformation. But both the intensity and the exact constellations of these problems, as

[14] S. M. Lipset, *Political Man* (Garden City, N.Y.: Doubleday & Company, Inc., 1960).

well as the degrees and ways of their regulation or solution, seem to vary greatly—although certainly not unsystematically—among different modern societies.

DIFFERENT HISTORICAL STARTING POINTS AND ORIENTATIONS OF MODERNIZING ELITES

How, then, can this great structural variety attendant on modernization be explained?

One crucial variable which may explain this variety is the fact that various societies have different starting points of modernization.[15] As already indicated, the process of modernization may take off from tribal groups (usually in colonial set-ups), from caste societies, from different types of peasant societies, and from societies with different degrees and types of prior urbanization. These groups may vary greatly with regard to the extent to which they have various flexible, differentiated resources, be they capital or manpower resources or identification with broader collectivities. Their abilities for the setting up and implementation of relatively differentiated goals, may vary, or their ability for dealing with the new problems that they face internally and in relation to other groups, and the extent to which they are willing or able to become integrated into new, wider social frameworks.

But even in those cases, when these broader strata evince some propensity for modernization, the intensity of this orientation may vary greatly among different societies—and thus may greatly influence the concrete structural features of their modernization. Thus, to quote Gerschenkorn, one of the pioneers of this approach:

The map of Europe in the nineteenth century showed a motley picture of countries varying with regard to the degree of their economic backwardness. At the same time, processes of rapid industrialization started in several of those countries from very different levels of economic backwardness. Those differences in points—or planes—of departure, were of crucial significance for the nature of the subsequent development. Depending on a given country's degree of economic backwardness on the eve of its industrialization, the course and character of the latter tended to vary in a number of important respects. Those variations can be readily compressed into the shorthand of six propositions:

1. The more backward a country's economy, the more likely was its industrialization to start discontinuously as a sudden great spurt proceeding at a relatively high rate of growth of manufacturing output.

2. The more backward a country's economy, the more pronounced was the stress in its industrialization on bigness of both plant and enterprise.

3. The more backward a country's economy, the greater was the stress upon producers' goods as against consumers' goods.

4. The more backward a country's economy, the greater was the part played

[15] Eisenstadt, *Modernization, Growth and Diversity.*

by special institutional factors designed to increase supply of capital to the nascent industries and, in addition, to provide them with less decentralized and better informed entrepreneurial guidance; the more backward the country, the more pronounced was the coerciveness and comprehensiveness of those factors.

5. The more backward a country's economy, the heavier the pressure upon the levels of consumption of the population.

6. The more backward a country, the less likely was its agriculture to play any active role by offering to the growing industries the advantages of an expanding industrial market based in turn on the rising productivity of "agricultural labor." [16]

These propositions can be applied not only to the economic sphere, but to all major institutional spheres. Thus, for instance, in the political field, the lack of any long-standing frameworks of political communities may explain development, in connection with wide political recruitment of relatively monolithic parties, or preponderance of bureaucratic organizations. Or the lack of wider political interests and orientation within the broader groups and strata may facilitate the development of small, militant, intellectual sects set on a total transformation of society.

Of no smaller importance than the initial starting point of modernization, however, is the nature of the impetus which gives the initial push to modernization, whether it is generated through the internal activities of various groups and elites or through the impact of various external forces such as colonial and imperial expansion, spread of technical innovations or of cultural movements.

The nature of such initial push may greatly influence the relative temporal sequence of modernization in different institutional spheres, whether it takes place first in the economic, the political, the cultural, or the ecological (e.g., urbanization) sphere.

But the great variety of structural forms accompanying the process of modernization in different countries is influenced not only by the resources and orientations of the various social groups and strata or by the nature of the initial push to modernization. Any such level of resources or type of orientations may be, as it were, directed or molded in different ways—and the exact way in which it is so molded depends to no small extent, although certainly not entirely, on the policies of the more active elites of a society, of those groups that have been called the "modernization elites." It is here that the second major new approach comes in.

Most pertinent and basic in this context is Shils' analysis of different institutional patterns of modern and modernizing societies—political democracy, tutelary democracy, modernizing oligarchy, totalitarian oli-

---

[16] A. Gerschenkorn, *Economic Backwardness in Historical Perspective* (Cambridge, Mass.: Harvard University Press, 1962).

garchy, and traditional oligarchy—which shows how the crystallization of each such type is influenced not only by the broad structural conditions of these societies but also to a very large degree by the composition and orientation of the leading elites in each type of society.[17]

Similarly Kerr and his associates' recent analysis has shown, even if in a preliminary way, that different elites tend to develop different strategies with regard to some major problems of social and economic policy, such as the pace of industrialization, sources of funds, priorities in development, pressures on enterprises and managers, the educational system, policies of agriculture, methods of allocation of labor, and many others.[18] This insight of theirs can be, as we shall see, generalized to other spheres.

Such approach which emphasizes the importance of elites in the process of modernization basically assumes—although the full implication of its assumption has not always been made explicit—that the process of modernization is, like so many other types of creation of new institutional structures, borne or pushed by "charismatic" groups or personalities, even if the characteristics and orientations of these groups differ greatly from those of older, classical religious types of charisma; and that what may be called the institutionalization of modernization is not unlike the processes of routinization of charisma which were analyzed by Max Weber.[19]

Such elites may differ greatly in several basic respects crucial for the process of modernization.[20] First of all, they may differ in their attitude to modernity, in their acceptance or resistance to the changes inherent in it and especially in the extent to which they may envisage such change in modern and not traditional terms—i.e., in terms of system transformation and not of small changes limited only to one sphere, such as the technical or military one, and aiming only at making the traditional system more efficient. Whatever their attitude to modernity, they may also differ in the deliberateness of this attitude of theirs; in the extent to which they tend to conceive it as a conscious goal that has to be implemented through organized action. These two need not always go together. Often elites that were open to modernity, were even the main harbinger of modernity, did not envisage such changes in terms of conscious goals for the implementation of which special organizations had to be established.

Such elites may also differ greatly in the extent to which they are able to adapt to changes generated outside of themselves, and in the extent

[17] Shils, *op. cit.*
[18] C. Kerr, *Industrialism and Industrial Man* (Cambridge, Mass.: Harvard University Press, 1960).
[19] Weber, *The Theory of Social and Economic Organization,* pp. 363-85.
[20] Shils, *op. cit.*

to which they are ready to cooperate with other elites in the processes of modernization. The combination of these variables may explain to no small degree the structural variety attendant on modernization.

STRUCTURAL DIVERSITY AND CONDITIONS OF SUSTAINED GROWTH

But this still leaves open the question of the conditions of sustained growth, of the conditions under which a society not only undergoes continual changes and growing structural differentiation, develops mass-consensual tendencies, and even accepts modernity with its emphasis on progress and change, but also develops an institutional structure capable of dealing with new, changing problems and of absorbing, within its central institutional sphere, new social groups and strata with their problems and demands.

What then are the conditions conducive to the development of such growth-sustaining structure? Are they in any way related to the development, the structural varieties found in different modern or modernizing societies? Does there exist any relation between the scope of differentiation and social mobilization and the capacity for sustained growth? Are some types of social structure—of class structure, of different types of organization—better adapted to the problem of system transformation than others?

Also of crucial importance is the problem of the relation between Westernization and modernization—a problem of the extent to which non-Western societies may develop all the characteristics of modernity without becoming Westernized in the cultural sense, without adapting the concrete cultural and organizational forms of modernity as they developed in the Western countries, even if these countries were the first to have become modernized.

Many researches that took off from the preceding considerations led to or were based on the assumption, usually implicit, that the conditions for sustained growth, for continuous development and modernization in different institutional fields, are depended on or tantamount to continual extension of these various socio-demographic and/or structural indices of modernization. According to this view, the more a society exhibits or develops the basic characteristics of structural specialization and the higher it is on various indices of social mobilization, the less traditional and the more modern it would be; that is, by implication the better it would be able to develop continuously, to deal continuously with new problems and social forces and to develop a continuously expanding institutional structure.[21]

Closely related to the preceding approach were the assumptions of the

[21] B. F. Hoselitz, "Noneconomic Factors in Economic Development," *American Economic Review*, 47 (May 1957), 28-71.

primacy of the economic sphere in development and modernization, of the central importance of the economic solvent for the development of viable modern societies and political regimes and of the relative assurance of the continuity of modernization, of sustained growth, of continuous development in any institutional sphere—be it economics, politics, or social organization—after the initial "take-off." [22]

The examination of these assumptions may prove useful as a starting point in the analysis of processes of modernization—but, as we shall see, only as a starting point. In the following chapter we shall present a series of analyses of some major types of modernizing societies focusing on the analysis of the condition that facilitates or impedes the development of an institutional system capable of such continuous sustained growth.

[22] W. W. Rostow, *The Stages of Economic Growth* (London: Cambridge University Press, 1960).

Using the major variables in the analysis of modernization presented above—the various indices of modernization, its different historical starting points, the attitudes of modernizing elites, and the temporal sequence of processes of modernization—we proceed to the analysis of some of its major patterns, with the aim of understanding some of the reasons for their structural variety as well as, and especially, the conditions conducive to sustained growth as against conditions of regression and breakdowns.

It would, of course, be beyond the scope of this book to analyze even in a preliminary way all the major types or patterns of modernization and all the major elements that go into the construction of such types, but some general indications may not be out of place. These indications can be arranged according to the two major aspects of modernization—on the one hand the continuous structural differentiation, the impingement of broader groups on the center, and the problems arising out of these processes, and on the other the ability of the centers to deal with these problems, to develop adequate contractual and precontractual arrangements and symbols alike. It might be worth while to distinguish first

CHAPTER FOUR

Patterns Developing in the First Phase of Modernization

between two phases of modernization according to the scope of mobilization, then to cross them with the nature of the existing or emerging centers.

The most important structural characteristics of the first, "limited" phase, which developed in the late eighteenth and nineteenth centuries in Europe (especially western Europe, the United States, and to a smaller extent in Latin America and the Asian countries) are: the relatively small scale of the scope of various new organizations; the development of many relatively specific, goal-oriented organizations; the development of as yet restricted markets and for free-floating resources in the major institutional spheres; and the relative predominance of "public" —representation, communal, or professional—regulative and allocative arrangements.

At this phase the upper and middle classes have usually been predominant in the active process of modernization, which was gradually extended to the wider groups and strata, through the relatively slow and gradual tempo of urbanization and industrialization.

The most general problems arising at this phase of modernization have been the ways in which these broader groups and strata can be drawn into the central institutions of society, the ways in which their various problems crystallized into orientations of protest and political demands and then became "translated" into various policies which extended the scope of the central institution of the society, and the extent to which at the center there did indeed develop cohesive frameworks and new, flexible, collective identities.

These general problems can be subdivided into several areas. The first was the extension of political participation—both formal (i.e., franchise) and more general actual participation in the community in terms of access to various positions of power, on the one hand, and the ability to influence policy-making and decisions on the other.

Second were the various problems attendant on the growing transformation of the cultural-collective identity from a traditional ascriptive one to a more secular, differentiated civil and national one, and the consequent problems of the extent to which it was possible to incorporate the various traditions of different groups in the new symbolic center.

The third broad area of problems accrued from the first upsurge of industrialization and urbanization. It was here that the whole gamut of social problems, as well as more articulate social and political demands connected with them, developed.

The way in which these problems were dealt with varied greatly according to the orientation of the major modernization elites and the initial pushes to modernization—and were most evident in the structure organization and symbols of the new center.

The center of the society which tended to develop at this stage of mobilization has usually, although not always, been characterized by the development of some strong, modern centralized political frameworks and sometimes also of relatively new differentiated central symbols, before the onset of industrialization and the rapid extension of political aspirations to wider groups and strata.

But such centers have differed greatly according to their strength and flexibility, according to the extent to which they tend to retain rigid traditional orientations, and according to their ability to deal with the various problems analyzed above. These differences have been, as we shall see in greater detail later, of great importance from the point of view of the whole process of modernization.

The characteristics and problems of the second phase of modernization differ in several important aspects from those of the first.

The most basic characteristics of this phase of modernization are the growing "mass" aspect; i.e., the spread of participation in all the major spheres of society to broader groups and strata and a continuous direct and intensive impact of these broader groups on the various centers of society.

Structurally this phase of growing tempo of social mobilization was first characterized by the growth of large-scale and multi-purpose specialized—i.e., nonecological and nonkinship—groups and associations. Second, it is characterized by the continuous extension and interpenetration of the various internal markets in the institutional spheres of the society. Third, it is characterized by the continually growing and spreading urbanization and by the continual spread of mass media of communication.

At this stage there develop very important differences between societies—to no small degree identical with the distinctions between "old-timers" and "newcomers" to modernization. Structurally the major difference between these two types of societies was that between the *continuation* of relatively gradual, although often uneven, social mobilization, industrialization, and economic growth, and the consequent impingement of the broader strata into already existing and established frameworks, on the one hand; and the process of a relatively quick tempo of social mobilization and the direct intensive impingement of this process on the very establishment of the new centers, on the other.

In the latter case this process was often connected with a different pattern of the tempo of social mobilization and of the relative temporal development of the modernization in different institutional spheres. In most of the new states the process of differentiation and social mobilization was stronger in the political, ecological, and educational sphere than in the industrial or economic one. The phenomenon frequently found in many of these societies of overurbanization unaccompanied by industrialization is a very important indication of this general trend.

Side by side with the older types of social problems and orientations of protest and political demands some new ones tend to arise, and their nature differs greatly between the relative "oldtimers" and "newcomers" to modernization. In the older societies this second phase brought two interconnected problems. One was the possibility of the split-up of the center between different modernized groups and elites, the development of divisive symbols and orientations, and the consequent breakdown of relatively developed modernized frameworks. The other was the possibility of growing apathy of broader strata toward the center, and/or the withering away of the center under the pressure of various populist tendencies.

Among the relative newcomers there developed, in addition, the problem of their ability to establish effective central institutions and symbols under the impact of continually growing pressure of diverse groups that had not themselves undergone adequate processes of structural transformation and self-modernization. Moreover, among many of the new countries the problem of forging out a new national identity was very closely connected with problems of encounter between the impact of western European culture and with the necessity to justify their national tradition in terms at least to some extent congruent with these new, modern Western orientations.

Here again the solutions to these problems—and the consequent ability of the new centers to deal adequately with problems of sustained change —varied greatly according to the internal cohesion and orientation of the major modernizing elites.

In the forthcoming chapters we shall start with the brief analysis of the early cases of modernization, especially in Europe and also in Japan, which were initially cases of relatively limited modernization, differentiating among them according to the flexibility and strength of their centers. We shall also deal briefly with some of the problems attendant on their transition to the second stage of modernization. We shall then proceed to analyze in somewhat greater length cases of the second phase of modernization, emphasizing especially, but not exclusively, the latecomers.

In each case we shall examine how the nature and orientations of the major modernizing elites and attitudes of the major strata and the structure of the center have influenced the process of modernization and its structural characteristics, and the extent of the ability of the emerging institutional structure to deal within the continually changing social problems and orientation of protest.

Patterns of Continuous, Pluralistic Modernization in Western Europe, the United States and the Dominions

THE MODERNIZING ELITES AND ORIENTATIONS

We shall start with the first type of modern regimes; those which have developed, in a gradual way, in western Europe,[1] England,[2] The Netherlands,[3] the Scandinavian countries,[4] the United States,[5] and in the English-speaking Dominions.[6]

It was in these European countries that the first historical processes of modernization developed, mostly through the transformation and working of various internal forces in these societies, and only to a small extent through the impact of external events.

On the eve of modernization, in the sixteenth and seventeenth centuries, these societies were characterized by a relatively high level of differentiation in general and of technological development in particular. They were composed of relatively differentiated and complex groups and strata, such as various landed aristocracies, diversified peasantry, and strong religious groups and organizations, and by a steadily growing urban population with strong traditions of corporate autonomy on the one hand and relatively strong political—usually monarchical—centers on the other.

The process of modernization started in these societies more or less simultaneously both at the center and from within the broader social strata. At the center the process of initial modernization was developed by strong absolute monarchs—the Tudors in England, the Vasas in Sweden, to a smaller extent William the Silent in Holland—and/or by limited oligarchic groups, such as the urban patriciates in Holland, which tended continually to incorporate new active social elements from wider strata.[7] In most of these countries these new centers and the

---

[1] D. Thomson, *Europe since Napoleon* (New York: Alfred A. Knopf, Inc., 1962); T. Cole, ed., *European Political Systems* (New York: Alfred A. Knopf, Inc., 1961); and S. H. Beer and A. B. Ulam, eds., *Patterns of Government: The Major Political Systems of Europe* (New York: Random House, Inc., 1962).

[2] D. Thomson, *The Democratic Ideal in England and France* (London: Macmillan & Co., Ltd., 1943).

[3] P. Geyl, *The Revolt of the Netherlands* (New York: Barnes & Noble, Inc., 1958).

[4] D. R. Rustow, "Scandinavia," in S. Neumann, ed., *Modern Political Parties* (Chicago: University of Chicago Press, 1956), pp. 169-94.

[5] S. M. Lipset, *The First New Nation: The United States in Historical and Comparative Perspective* (New York: Basic Books, Inc., Publishers, 1963).

[6] R. Taft, "Australia," in A. M. Rose, ed., *The Institutions of Advanced Societies* (Minneapolis: University of Minnesota Press, 1958).

[7] M. Beloff, *The Age of Absolutism: 1660-1815* (London: Hutchinson & Co. (Publishers), Ltd., 1954).

centralized political frameworks became transformed and reorganized not only in the administrative field but also in the symbolic and broader political fields. They developed new, more flexible nontraditional symbols which legitimized continuous widening of political participation, emphasizing their common attachment to the new center and potential participation in it.[8] Moreover, the establishment of these new centers entailed in many countries, especially the Protestant ones, incorporation of new, transcendental orientations which served as bases of new, wider universalistic commitments, binding the rulers and ruled in new normative relations.[9] The English Glorious Revolution is perhaps the best illustration of this trend, parallels to which can be also found in Holland and to a lesser extent in Scandinavia. Parallel to this, more flexible central political institutions, such as legislatures, modern executives, and later the continuously expanding central bureaucratic administration tended to develop.

Although in almost all these societies the establishment of a modern central framework was connected with some revolutionary phase or event—the Great Rebellion and the Glorious Revolution in England, the Revolt of the Netherlands in the sixteenth century, and the American Revolution—yet this revolutionary phase neither caused a sharp break with the past nor gave rise to a sharp and continuous cleavage in the central symbols of the political community. The pre-existing institutional-political structure was relatively flexible, so that it was able to incorporate within its orbit and frameworks some of the new symbols and demands.

This process of setting up the initial modern political frameworks and symbols has taken place in somewhat different ways in the United States and the Dominions. In the United States a new polity was created by an act of revolution or rebellion which resulted in a break from the preceding political sphere.[10] But even this break was legitimized in terms of values that were not entirely different from those of the former political system, and it was at first borne by a relatively small oligarchic group which was able to crystallize new central symbols of political identity and institution. But here the tempo of participation of broader groups in the society became much quicker, and hence also the possibility increased of more populist outbreaks and movements of protest.

Side by side with such transformation and development of the centers,

[8] S. Neumann, "Germany: Changing Patterns and Lasting Problems," in Neumann, ed., *Modern Political Parties* (Chicago: University of Chicago Press, 1956), pp. 354-94.

[9] Lipset, *op. cit.;* D. Thomson, *England in the Nineteenth Century* (London: Pelican Books, 1960); Rustow, *op. cit.*, pp. 169-94; and Geyl, *op. cit.*

[10] Lipset, *ibid.* For an interesting comparison of the United States and Europe, see also S. P. Huntington, "Political Modernization and America vs. Europe," *World Politics,* 18 (April 1966), 378-415.

there developed in these societies various modernizing tendencies and processes among wider strata.[11] The major locus of these modernizing tendencies of the broader groups were the various so-called "middle groups," especially the urban groups, and to some extent also some aristocratic as well as some upper peasant groups. Within these broad strata the more intensive modernizing impulses were located among various secondary elites, which were initially most active in the religious, cultural, and economic spheres. Most important among such elites were the various Protestant groups, active intellectual centers of which developed throughout Europe in the period of the Renaissance, and the more active entrepreneurial-economic groups; trading, banking, and early industrial groups.[12]

They often utilized or expanded the opportunities for economic growth provided by the initial high level of economic differentiation and technology. Of special importance in the economic context was the relatively speedy transformation of agriculture and of the rural sectors, and their incorporation into various modern frameworks in the developing market economy.

The general trend of economic modernization was that of capitalist-commercial and later individual development based on these entrepreneurial classes, in close relation with the "classical" liberal professions (law, medicine), later expanding itself to new working groups, incorporating them into the new industrial civilization.

These groups were also greatly helped in the continual expansion of their economic, religious, and intellectual activities by the relatively great flexibility of the pre-existing political centers. One of the most salient characteristics of the process of modernization in these societies was a relatively high degree of compatibility between the modernizing orientations that developed from within the center and the broader groups and strata.

Side by side with these specific orientations of the more active modernizing elites, there gradually also tended to develop relatively autonomous modernizing orientations among the broader strata,[13] especially among urban middle and working classes. These orientations were initially also often based on religious transformations (as, for instance, among the Methodist and other "nonconformist" groups), and on growing participation in the expanding industrial system, and later on ex-

---

[11] M. Weber, *The Protestant Ethic and the Spirit of Capitalism*, trans. T. Parsons (New York: Charles Scribner's Sons, 1958); R. H. Tawney, *Religion and the Rise of Capitalism* (London: John Murray, 1929); and F. Venturi, *The Roots of Revolution* (New York: Alfred A. Knopf, Inc., 1960).

[12] J. Bowle, *The Unity of European History* (London: Jonathan Cape, Ltd., 1949), pp. 170-225.

[13] S. Burrell, "Calvinism, Capitalism and the Middle Classes: Some Afterthoughts on an Old Problem," *Journal of Modern History*, 32 (1960), 129-41.

panded to social activity in various local and union affairs. By virtue of these characteristics the wider groups and strata were to a very great extent open to modernizing influences and tendencies in both economic and ideological spheres, and were gradually drawn into the newly emerging wider economic and cultural frameworks and into the orbit of the new central political institutions.

Perhaps one of the most important aspects of these processes was the development, among most of these groups, of very specific types of new, flexible status orientation. These can be perhaps most clearly discerned among many of the active Protestant entrepreneurial groups.

These evinced a combination of two characteristics or orientations. First was their "openness" toward the wider social structure—rooted in their "this-worldly" orientations, which were not limited only to the economic sphere, but which gradually extended also into demands for wider political participation and for setting up of new, wider political frameworks and criteria. Second, they were characterized by a certain combination of autonomy and self-sufficiency from the point of view of their status orientation with openness to the broader society. Unlike groups or societies with more autocratic or aristocratic status tradition, they evinced but little dependence—from the point of view of the crystallization of their status symbols—on the existing (i.e., monarchical or ecclesiastical) centers of political power. Here also the maintenance and institutionalization of these status orientations was to no small degree due not only to the internal orientations of these various groups, but also to the flexibility or "openness" of the existing political and cultural centers.

TEMPORAL SEQUENCE AND STRUCTURAL CHARACTERISTICS
OF MODERNIZATION

The processes analyzed above gave rise to some specific patterns of temporal sequence of the process of modernization in different institutional spheres and different specific structural characteristics of the continually developing social structure.

This sequence was characterized first of all by a relatively slow tempo and by stronger development of modern organizations and symbols at the center of the society than in the periphery. Second, it was characterized by the growth of relatively strong and flexible central modern political frameworks before the development of widespread industrialization and politization, and by the drawing in of wider groups and strata into new urban and industrial spheres, before they became politically active and developed high levels of aspiration and effective demands in the political and economic spheres.[14]

[14] See Thomson, *Europe since Napoleon;* and the analysis of European political systems in books mentioned in footnote 1.

They were first politically organized in interest groups and social movements, which later became integrated to some extent into political parties and became capable of making articulate demands on the central political sphere.[15]

However, the major changes in the political distribution of power within the new transformed center reflected gradually, even in the beginning, the changes in economic structure—which provided in many ways the impetus to the developments in these new central frameworks, to which the rulers responded even before the new strata became politically articulate.

Most of the broader strata, ranging from aristocracy through the middle sectors and down to the various workers' groups, evinced a relatively high degree of status flexibility and openness to new elements.[16] These developments were facilitated and in turn reinforced by the internal cohesiveness of both middle and workers' groups, and by their ability to cope internally with at least some of the problems of modernization, as evinced in the development of numerous social and political activities on the local and plant (industrial) levels.

The temporal lag between the tempo of modernization in the center and in the periphery has minimized, except in rather extreme and temporary cases, the direct impact of various manifestations of social disorganization and of eruption of social problems on the central political activities, symbols, and orientations. In most cases a gradual linking took place between relatively differentiated frameworks in the center— such as the parliamentary organizations and various organs of political and cultural activity—and the relatively small-scale activities and various professional, middle, and working-class groups and associations in the periphery. This was, in turn, connected with the development of a relatively high degree of predominance of public, voluntary self-regulative groups, in the form of various voluntary associations and professional and trade union organizations, cutting across various strata and more specific structural organizations. These did not become entirely weakened with growth of the scale of differentiation and of the major units of social and economic activities and organizations, and with the transition to bureaucratization in the economic and political spheres.

ABSORPTION OF CHANGE IN THE
PLURALISTIC-CONSTITUTIONAL REGIMES

The different combinations of the various factors analyzed above— the institutional placement of the innovating groups, the flexibility of

---

[15] Rustow, *op. cit.*

[16] Thomson, *England in the Nineteenth Century;* and Thomson, *The Democratic Ideal in England and France.*

the existing political structure and the relative openness of the wider social strata to modernizing tendencies, on the one hand, and the different temporal sequences of modernization and their structural characteristics, on the other—greatly influenced the types of modern regime which developed in the Western countries. This was the constitutional-pluralistic pattern of modern regimes—the pattern in which the potentialities and tendencies of mass-consensual societies based on civility became most fully, although certainly imperfectly, realized.

Within these regimes has developed an almost unconscious ability to absorb change; that is, they have developed an institutional framework and a general political style and set of attitudes which proved to be favorable to the absorption of social and political change.[17]

Within most of these regimes the capacity to absorb changing political demands and organizations usually has not a *fully conscious* political goal. The goal has rather been attained—insofar as it is attained—through the flexibility of the political institutions and through the sensitivity of the major political and social elites to the continually changing demands and forms of political organization. Although obviously the rulers (and those who compete for the formulation and implementation of policies) initiate political reforms and changes and articulate the major policies, yet the initial crucial impetus to such changes usually comes in these regimes from within the fold of various social, professional, or cultural groups, from different interest groups, social movements, from the more diffuse general public opinion, and from the political elites that appeal to such groups, compete for their support, and attempt to integrate them in the framework of political parties.

It is this impetus that becomes translated through the active participation and articulation of the various competing elites into various, often innovating, policies and into new institutional frameworks.

In this way, political innovations tend in these societies to be initiated and articulated by political leadership (be it the leadership of a party or of a more independent group) and by different parties which absorb the impulses for change from within the public, from wider social groups and strata, and which mobilize wider support from various goals and policies.

The major areas of political decision making and of institutionalization of political changes and innovations are usually centered, at least formally, in the legislature, in the executive acting in the legislature, and to some extent also in the bureaucracy. It is in these more central organs that the major policies are, if not decided on, at least fully and publicly articulated, decided, and defended.

True enough, the importance both of mass parties and bureaucracies

17 See footnote 9.

as arenas of decision making has been growing steadily with growing differentiation of the social structure and with continuous modernization; and many crucial political decisions and functions have become concentrated within them in all modern regimes, constitutional or totalitarian.

But in the constitutional regimes neither the parties nor the bureaucracy have become the *only* areas of political discussion and innovation, and executive and legislative·organs continued to maintain some of their positions of control, at least symbolic, as the main frameworks of independent public opinion and leadership, and the main areas in which political innovation became institutionalized.

The innovating ability of the democratic elites and the possibility of institutionalizing various innovations were to no small degree dependent on the ability of the parties and their leadership to integrate various diverging interest groups, and to institutionalize the more intensive demands and orientations of social movements, and consequently also the continuous existence and political ability of some independent leadership and public opinion.

This pattern of absorption of change was also closely related to the nature of the major types of articulation of political demands that tended to develop within these societies, which were characterized by a gradual interlinking of concrete and discrete interest groups and of more totalistically oriented social movements into the frameworks of relatively flexible parties or partylike political organizations, and by the relative importance of public opinion (based on voluntary associations and various public bodies) as an important interlinking between the various parties.[18]

In order to understand more fully the working of these regimes, it might be worth while to analyze the movements and orientations of protest that developed in them and the ways in which they were handled.

MOVEMENTS OF PROTEST AND PATTERNS OF ERUPTIONS

The structure and organization of the major symbols and movements of protest was, in these countries, focused on several aspects of the social and cultural order, especially on problems relating to the new political center—economic and social problems, extent and scope of political participation—and on issues deriving from the new industrial order of the cultural order, especially those of religious freedom and toleration.

It was in these regimes that there first developed the specifically modern types of political organization—sociopolitical movements and political parties—which tended to focus around these various issues.

[18] M. Kaplan, ed., *The Revolution in World Politics* (New York: John Wiley & Sons, Inc., 1962), esp. Parts I, XI.

It was here that the first social, national, or conservative movements and parties developed. It was in these countries that the first relatively clear-cut distinction developed between "left" and "right" in the usual sense, i.e., between those who hold the privileged positions and those who aspire to change the existing arrangement of political, social, and economic privileges, and to broaden levels in distribution and access to them.[19]

But these issues were usually relatively dispersed, both in time and among different groups of the population. Only rarely did there develop movements in which political, social, economic, and cultural divisions coalesced so as to create total rifts among groups and strata.[20]

Moreover, different issues came up in different periods of time. Thus, for instance, issues of the spread of political participation were settled before the onset of problems stemming from industrialization and class division, but rarely coincided with cultural or religious ones. Similarly, these movements were but rarely—and then only for short periods of time—totalistic and oriented to the total overthrow of the existing regime. On the whole these organizations of protest evinced a relatively high degree of propensity to become incorporated into more integrated parties or partylike organizations, while maintaining also some of their own autonomy and orientations.[21]

This relatively successful continual absorption of changing problems and demands was mainly effected through the execution and implementation of various social, economic, and cultural policies which were addressed to the major problems that developed in these societies.

First there developed in these countries policies dealing with political problems proper—with a continuous extension of the suffrage on the local and central level, and the facilitation of the growing participation of wider strata in the various spheres of the society.

In the social, economic, and educational fields varied policies gradually developed aiming at the restriction of the free play of economic forces; at assurance of some minimal social security to broader strata of the population; at effecting regulation of conditions of work in industrial enterprises; and at the provision of varied social services.[22]

In the cultural sphere we find a relatively continuous flexibility of the

[19] P. Robertson, *Revolutions of 1848: A Social History* (New York: Harper & Row, Publishers, 1960); and S. M. Lipset, "Socialism: Left and Right, East and West," *Confluence,* 5, 7 (1958).

[20] Neumann, ed., *op. cit.*

[21] Thomson, *England in the Nineteenth Century;* and Thomson, *Europe since Napoleon.*

[22] C. Kerr, *Industrialism and Industrial Man* (Cambridge, Mass.: Harvard University Press, 1960); H. L. Wilensky and C. N. Lebeaux, *Industrial Society and Social Welfare* (New York: Russell Sage Foundation, 1958), esp. pp. 138-52, 250-75; and H. I. Clarke, *Social Legislation* (New York: Appleton-Century-Crofts, 1957), pp. 437-63.

central institutions and symbols which enabled them to override several crucial points of tension—such as those between religious prescription and freedom (or toleration), or between religion and secularism—and the incorporation of some aspects of revolutionary symbols (such as ideas of liberty of the subject, equality before the law) into the central symbols of the society. At the same time there also took place the inclusion or incorporation of some of the more particularistic symbols, such as various regional and sectorial ones, into the new, central symbols.

It was this process that forged these societies as the first mass-consensual ones based on a framework of civil order, and assured their relative continuity.

In general we find in these societies a gradual extension and widening of the participation of wider strata in the central institution of the society —not only in formal terms, but also in terms of accessibility to the central institutional political and cultural frameworks. This growing participation was usually attained through some struggle or pressures on the center by these various strata, which were continually transformed and which evinced both a relatively high degree of cohesion and ability for self-regulation and an active and potentially cooperative attitude to participation in the central institutions.

But needless to say, in these as in any other societies, processes tended to develop that could have undermined this process of continuous absorption. The various eruptions to which these regimes were subject tended mostly to develop in proportion to the degree to which the parties or partylike organizations were not able to assure an adequate integration of interest groups and social movements within their frameworks. Such more extreme eruptions and activities developed both on the left, whether in socialist or anarchist form, and on the right, whether in the form of traditional conservative or more populistic and nationalistic forms.

The nature and organizational contents of the eruptions that tended to develop in the constitutional regimes differ greatly according to the level of differentiation of their social structure and of the extension of political participation within it. Thus, in the early stages of modernization, when these regimes were ruled by relatively small oligarchies and when political participation was limited, most of the eruptions took on the form of relatively unorganized, highly activistic movements and outlines oriented to the attainment either of immediate needs or of political rights and inclusion in the body politic.

With growing extension of social differentiation and political participation, more organized eruptions tended to develop, in the form of either various social and/or populist movements or of organized interest groups.[23]

---

[23] Kaplan, ed., *op. cit.*, esp. Part II, "Politics and Movements in Developed Areas."

This tendency to more organized eruptions has been rooted in the fact that by their very nature such regimes encourage certain levels of articulation and organization of political demands and of mobilization and organization of political support. The eruptions that tend to develop within these regimes derive their strength more from the lack of absorption of such demands by the existing political institution than from the nonavailability of any type of leadership to organize and articulate such demands, although in some instances—especially, but not only, in the initial stages of modernization—cases of lack of any adequate leadership, of erosion of the active political leadership, may also develop within these regimes. But on the whole they evinced a high level of propensity, while maintaining their own autonomy, to become incorporated into more organized parties or organizations.

Side by side with these more organized and articulated types of protest pockets of apathy and of social problems and protest tended to develop, becoming continually institutionalized as sorts of subcultures within these societies.

There may also easily develop, within the western societies, a growing general apathy towards wider social and cultural orientations, an erosion of such wider commitments, a tendency among many broader groups only to make demands on the center without developing strong commitment to it, or to broader cultural orientations.

This has become especially important in later stages of modernization and industrialization and, paradoxically enough, with the institutionalization of welfare state policies. This institutionalization created possibilities of development of pockets of social problems, relative poverty, and unemployment on the one hand and overall apathy on the other, which while becoming even more segregated from the center, yet developed and coalesced into continuous subcultures which could perhaps erode many of the more active orientations and feelings of identity participation of certain groups in the society.

Perhaps one of the most paradoxical developments in this context was that the very steady economic expansion tended often to worsen the lot of some deprived lower groups and strata and to minimize their effective accessibility to the new frameworks.[24] Moreover, intensive social and economic development often dislocated various groups, especially lower- and middle-class ones, and made them feel alienated from the central frameworks, and facilitated the development of populistic tendencies.

---

[24] Thomson, *Europe since Napoleon;* W. Petersen, ed., *American Social Patterns* (Garden City, N.Y.: Doubleday & Company, Inc., 1956), esp. chap. by M. Deutsch and M. E. Collins, "Interracial Housing," pp. 7-63; and J. Dollard, *Caste and Class in a Southern Town* (New York: Harper & Row, Publishers, 1949).

FRANCE AND ITALY—SOME COMPARATIVE NOTES

This specific configuration of the western European and the United States patterns of modernization can be more fully understood by comparing them, even if very briefly, with those of France,[25] and to some extent those of Italy.[26]

In France pre-existing political institutions, as epitomized in those of the absolutist monarchy of Louis XIV, were much less flexible than in England, Scandinavia, or The Netherlands. In Italy, initial modernization both in the Kingdom of Savoy and later in unified Italy was attained more by political and diplomatic maneuvers and by the activities of the certain parts of the bureaucratic groups—best represented by Cavour—than through the strength and activities of wider innovating social strata.

As a result, rather serious rifts developed in these countries in the central political symbols. Thus in France the Revolution created a continuous rift between the traditional and modern (revolutionary), aristocratic and republican, religious and secular orientations that persisted until the end of the Third Republic and even into the Fourth. In Italy several regions never became fully integrated into the new national frameworks set up around the House of Savoy. These rifts were to no small extent articulated and borne by different regional and professional elites, which tended also to perpetuate them through the establishment of special institutional frameworks, such as distinct schools and different family, educational, and professional traditions.

Side by side with these rifts there developed different patterns of temporal sequence of modernization, and some special structural characteristics. First, in France and Italy the scope of differentiation was much less evenly distributed between the different central and local levels, and the transition from one to another was abrupt and not continuous. At the center itself the impetus to modernization was stronger in administrative fields and weaker in cultural and economic ones and in the field of political participation proper.

Second, the tempo of social mobilization was uneven within parts of various groups and strata, such as the peasantry, the middle classes, etc., and the transition from small-scale to large-scale differentiation was much more abrupt. Many important groups—especially the traditional middle classes and various echelons or regions of the peasantry—tended to main-

[25] S. Hoffman, "Protest in Modern France," in Kaplan, ed., *op. cit.*, pp. 69-91; and J. R. Pitts, "Continuity and Change in Bourgeois France," in *In Search of France* (Cambridge, Mass.: Harvard University Center for International Affairs, 1963).

[26] Thomson, *Europe since Napoleon;* G. J. Magnone, "Italy," in Cole, ed., *op. cit.*, pp. 455-510; and R. Grew, "How Success Spoiled the Risorgimento," *Journal of Modern History,* **34**, 3 (September 1962), 238-55.

tain, in many regions (especially, but not only, in the south of Italy and France) traditional patterns of organizations, evincing but a weak inclination to modernize themselves and small ability to regulate their affairs in the new settings.

Hence a relatively higher extent of segregation of various social strata and groups tended to develop, and a much smaller extent of openness and crosscutting between them. The major meeting points and the regulative mechanisms between them were more imposed from the center, mainly through large-scale bureaucratic organizations.

Thus in both France and Italy there developed and crystallized more and more pockets of resistance to change and to modernization and different types of "delinquent communities" (i.e., communities not oriented to the attainment of their manifest goals; such as economic activities, professional services, and the like) tended to develop on almost all levels of the social structure. These often became crystallized both on a regional basis (as in the south of Italy) and/or on an economic or professional basis —especially, as has been pointed out, among traditional, professional, administrative, and later also workers' groups, on the one hand, and various peasant communities on the other.

In both these countries there tended to develop, to a very large extent, either discrete interest groups and/or social movements which remained relatively closed and which did not tend to become integrated into wider party political frameworks, and have therefore also greatly reinforced the divisive orientation of the various parties. These were fed to no small extent by temporal "spatial" coalescence of religious, cultural, and occupational cleavages.

Thus, for instance, in France religious and political or political and economic issues often tended to become prominent at the same time, as for instance in the 1848 Revolution and during the Paris Commune in 1870, and the class division between aristocracy and the bourgeoisie often corresponded with attitudes of loyalty or disloyalty to the political tradition of the French Revolution and of republicanism, or with the stand on the religious-secularism issue.

The movements of protest in these countries evinced greater susceptibility to ideological and organizational separativeness and evinced a smaller propensity to become integrated into more integrative and flexible party frameworks. Similarly, the organs of public opinion were relatively weak and were not always able to bridge adequately the various separate social and political groups.

In both countries the more extreme movements, both of the left and the right, with strong, populist admixtures, often tended to develop and played a rather constant role in the central social and political arenas, as constant focuses of eruptions, without becoming integrated into the central political process. This could be seen in the bourgeois parties and also in the organization of working class movements, in which various types of separatist (syndicalist) tendencies were very prominent.

Hence, on the whole these regimes evinced a smaller capacity to absorb change than the western European ones, even though in their broad institutional patterns they are relatively close. Although basically these regimes also evinced the major characteristics of mass-consensual order, yet already various disruptive tendencies undermining the civil order became very pronounced. The history of France in the nineteenth and twentieth centuries is characterized by continual rifts and instabilities, while in Italy the post-World War I crisis gave rise to the breakdown of the constitutional regime and the rise of the Fascist one.

The Spread of Modernization Beyond Western Europe

THE DEVELOPMENT OF SPLIT-UP MODERNIZATION

The western European modernization and its direct offshoots—that of the United States and the English-speaking Dominions—were the only cases of autochthonous and self-generating modernization; i.e., of modernization that developed mostly through the internal developments from within the society.

All the later cases of modernization took place in a different situation, in which the push to modernization came to no small degree from the outside, through the impingement of the new international political, economic, and intellectual systems that developed in wake of the initial changes in western Europe.

As modernization spread out first to central and eastern Europe and then to the Middle East, it did so to societies whose social backgrounds were different from those of the western European ones. Although some features of the common European tradition—landed nobility, commercial town centers—could also be found there, some crucial differences existed.

The general level of social differentiation and of technological development was much lower than in western Europe. The social pyramid was much steeper. The broad base of peasantry was wider, and further away from other groups. The more autonomous urban, religious, professional, or rural groups were less numerous and weaker, the rulers more autocratic.[27] The farther east one moved, the more the nobility became a service nobility, with little status autonomy or independent landed bases; the steeper grew the social pyramid; the lower the scope of autonomous urban institutions; the greater the initial importance of the state in technological and economic change and development. Moreover, in many of these socie-

[27] Neumann, ed., *op. cit.;* Cole, ed., *op. cit.;* Beer and Ulam, eds., *op. cit.;* and Thomson, *Europe since Napoleon.*

ties a sense of national unity did not develop in the initial stages of modernization, and nationalism itself became a political and cultural problem.[28]

As a result of all these factors a distinct, different pattern of initial modernization tended to develop in these societies.

The push to modernization was split up between different groups or institutional focuses in society, among which a greater degree of incompatibility and conflicts with regard to their modernizing tendencies developed.

At least two and often more different modernizing elites tended to develop, usually dissociated from one another. On the one hand there were the autocratic, traditional or semitraditional rulers—Peter the Great, Catherine the Great and her descendants in Russia, the Prussian kings, and later the Ottoman Sultans—bent on furthering controlled modernization limited to technical and some economic and administrative spheres. They were ready at most to abolish some feudal aspects of the social structure, such as peasant serfdom, but were unwilling to foster any more far-reaching changes that would assure the participation of broader groups in this political framework. On the other hand, there developed different modernizing groups, usually composed of intellectuals and some professionals and entrepreneurs, mostly rooted in weak and noncohesive social strata, themselves weak and isolated, with but tenuous mutual interrelations.

It was here that this special type of "intelligentsia" first developed as a special and crucial type of modernizing elite. Professional preachers and pamphleteers and schools were also important in the initial modernization in western Europe, but on the whole they quickly established close relations with the broader occupation strata, which shared some of their background and orientation. But the further east we move the more there develops an intelligentsia with but few firm roots in other occupational or social strata, alienated from them and the centers of power alike and very closed in itself. These intellectual groups tended to develop very intensive preoccupation with the problems of modernization on an ideological and political level, but were not very active in either the economic or civil sphere, thus reinforcing the mutual seclusiveness of these modernizing groups.

Consequently they were not very influential either in the central political institutions or the wider strata, whose internal transformation in the direction of modernization they were not usually able to generate. For their part, these broader groups were not able to develop the resources

[28] Royal Institute of International Affairs, *Nationalism* (London, 1940); H. Kohn, *The Idea of Nationalism: A Study in Its Origins and Background* (New York: The Macmillan Company, 1946); and E. Kedourie, *Nationalism* (London: Hutchinson & Co. (Publishers), Ltd., 1960).

for implementation of differentiated goals, nor were they willing or able to become incorporated and participate actively in the new, wider social and political frameworks. They tended to maintain their traditional petitioning activities or develop some discrete interest groups, but these were usually relatively inarticulate in terms of wider, differentiated political goals and did not become integrated into wider differentiated frameworks of political activities.

Many of these characteristics persisted also with growing urbanization and industrialization, evincing many of the characteristics of structural duality, which we shall analyze in greater detail later on. (See chapter on Latin America.)

AUTOCRATIC REGIMES—GERMANY AND RUSSIA

Beyond these very general characteristics, to some degree common to the various countries belonging to this broad type, there also developed many differences among them, according to the specific-modernizing orientation of their respective elites and broader groups, as well as in their interrelations. As it is not possible to dwell here on all such variations, we shall concentrate only on some outstanding cases.

At one extreme of such modern autocratic regimes we find the semi-autocratic regimes, such as the more traditional regimes of the nineteenth century (e.g., the Spanish and Portuguese ones [29]) or several of the eastern European regimes—Pilsudski's Poland or King Boris' Bulgaria—in the period between the two world wars.[30] These regimes have been characterized mainly by their attempt to minimize the level and development of social, economic, and political changes, even to the extent of the impediment of the full development of the major characteristics of modern political systems—e.g., extension of suffrage—and by the discouragement of more active tendencies of any modernizing groups or elites.

At the other extreme we find regimes such as that of Imperial Germany under Bismarck,[31] which can be seen as a mixed type in between the purely autocratic and the western European ones. Here there developed, first, a much greater extent of differentiation and development of various modern groups and strata, be they middle groups, economic entrepreneurs, intellectuals, or professionals—and, in terms of moderniz-

[29] Juan Linz, "An Authoritarian Regime: Spain," in E. Allardt and Y. Lettunen, eds., *Cleavages, Ideologies and Party Systems,* Transactions of the Westermark Society, 10 (Turku, 1964), pp. 292-343; and M. Derrick, *The Portugal of Salazar* (London: Campion Press, Ltd., 1959).

[30] C. E. Black, *The Establishment of Constitutional Government in Bulgaria* (Princeton, N.J.: Princeton University Press, 1943); and H. Seton-Watson, *Eastern Europe between the Wars: 1918-1941* (3rd ed.) (Hamden, Conn.: Shoe String Press, Inc., 1963).

[31] S. Neumann, "The German Political System," in Beer and Ulam, eds., *op. cit.*, pp. 468-596.

ing aims, much more active central elites, even if relatively traditional and autocratically oriented, epitomized in the personality of Bismarck.

These elites established modern unified political frameworks and at the same time aimed at industrialization of their countries; but on their own terms. They wanted to intensify the process of industrialization and of continuous social mobilization; but within frameworks of conservative national state and political order. While granting basic political and social rights to the citizen, they attempted to minimize the autonomous social transformation of these groups, especially of the workers: and they did not legitimize their autonomous social and political organization and expansion, nor their incorporation into the central symbolic and institutional system as equal parties or participants.

The modernizing orientations and activities of the more active broader social groups, although in many ways similar to some of the western European secondary elites, still tended to evince several distinct characteristics of their own.[32] First, most of these groups and strata were weaker in their political articulation and effectiveness and in their ability to effect transformation of the central political institutions. Second, and closely connected with the former, they were less autonomous in their status aspiration and perception, being still strongly oriented to the more aristocratic or "absolutistic" symbols of status. Hence they tended to maintain a greater extent of internal closeness, mutual divisiveness, and lack of internal flexibility—characteristics and orientations that they evinced also in the political field, especially in the ideologies and organization of the numerous political parties which developed throughout the nineteenth century, from the various bourgeois-liberal parties of the unsuccessful 1848 Revolution up to the later various democratic liberal and socialist parties of the Empire. At the same time they were not allowed by virtue of the Imperial constitution promulgated by Bismarck, to participate fully in central decision-making institutions, and hence also were denied the institutional facilities for breaking down their own closeness and divisiveness.

These tendencies of the social strata and political parties were in a way only intensified under the impact of the great and quick upsurge of industrialization and urbanization which took place from the last third of the nineteenth century on, under the aegis and control of the central executive and bureaucratic agencies. Under such conditions, indeed, alliances tended to develop between the autocratic elite and the various relatively modernized and differentiated groups and strata; especially the larger industrialist and financial groups, on the one hand, and the more organized workers on the other. But these alliances were based

[32] Kerr, op. cit.; D. C. McClelland, The Achieving Society (Princeton, N.J.: D. Van Nostrand Co., Inc., 1961); and E. Hagen, On the Theory of Social Change (Homewood, Ill.: Richard D. Irwin, Inc., 1962).

mostly on purely accommodative considerations and contractual arrangements, and were not fully bolstered up by new common precontractual ones, by new common flexible political and cultural symbols. Hence the level of cleavages and unsolved conflicts tended to rise continuously.[33]

Of special interest, of course, is the process of modernization in Russia.[34] Here the modernizing activities of the autocracy, while certainly less intensive than those of Germany, did expand continuously throughout the nineteenth century.

The intelligentsia, which constituted one of the major and focal modernizing elites, evinced a very high degree of closeness and but little ability to reach and interpenetrate wider groups and to help in their internal transformation and modernization. Similarly, the initially weak propensity of the middle strata to autonomous entrepreneurial activities and their dependence on the state emphasized their own weaknesses.

The workers' organizations that developed in these conditions were characterized by closure, divisiveness, and relatively small political autonomy and efficiency.

But even here some new, more promising beginning did take place at the end of the nineteenth century and the beginning of the twentieth. At that time these varied groups entered on a course of seeking out the possibility of establishing some new common social, cultural, and political frameworks. This course was impeded by the more regressive tendency of the autocracy after the revolution of 1905. Yet it may be that, but for the fortunes of war which have completely undermined the existing institutional framework, the course of Russia's later modernization might have taken on a different course than it did.

In eastern Europe and in the Middle East in the period between the two world wars, and also, as we shall see, in various Latin American countries, a great variety of different subtypes developed between these extreme subtypes of autocratic modernization regime, which, while sharing some of the characteristics of the split-up modernization, also evinced characteristics of their own. It would, however, be beyond the scope of our presentation here to analyze all of them in detail.[35]

[33] S. N. Eisenstadt, "Political Modernization: Some Comparative Notes," *International Journal of Comparative Sociology*, 5, 1 (March 1964), 3-24.

[34] M. Fainsod, *How Russia Is Ruled* (Cambridge, Mass.: Harvard University Press, 1955); Z. K. Brzezinski, *Ideology and Power in Soviet Politics* (New York: Frederick A. Praeger, Inc., 1962); J. A. Armstrong, *The Politics of Totalitarianism: The Communist Party of the Soviet Union from 1934 to the Present* (New York: Random House, Inc., 1961); and R. A. Feldmesser, "Social Class and Political Structure," in C. E. Black, ed., *The Transformation of Russian Society* (Cambridge, Mass.: Harvard University Press, 1960), pp. 235-53; also A. Inkeles, pp. 338 ff.

[35] Black, *op. cit.;* H. Seton-Watson, *op. cit.;* K. Karpat, *Turkey's Politics: The Transition to a Multi-Party System* (Princeton, N.J.: Princeton University Press, 1959); B. Lewis, *The Emergence of Modern Turkey* (London: Oxford University Press, 1961); and L. Binder, *The Ideological Revolution in the Middle East* (New York: John Wiley & Sons, Inc., 1964).

TEMPORAL SEQUENCE AND STRUCTURAL CHARACTERISTICS
IN SPLIT-UP MODERNIZATION

The patterns of temporal sequence of modernization, as well as their structural characteristics, that developed in the countries belonging to the broad type of split-up modernization evinced several specific characteristics. Here also the initial focus of modernization was in the political center; but the central political and administrative organs, created by the autocratic rulers, evinced but little capacity of symbolic transformation and of creation of new levels of political participation. These centers did not incorporate in their new symbols strong transcendental and universalistic orientations, which, as was the case in many of the western European countries, entailed a reformulation of the mutual bonds between rulers and ruled which provided the precontractual symbols for the development of new flexible and autonomous political and integrative institutions.

Economically these regimes were usually characterized by a relatively slow tempo of development from a rather traditional agrarian base, and by the attempts to overcome such retardation by special big spurts in railway construction and heavy industry.

Industrialization, therefore, took on special characteristics—such as concentration on heavy industry and the development of large-scale economic units—and was very heavily dependent on the activities and help of the central government.

This process of industrialization usually lagged behind the development of political and ideological demands and aspirations of small, intensive closed groups of intellectuals, but it came before the broader strata started to become modernized in the cultural or political field.

There was but little crosscutting or interpenetration between the major social strata, and each tended to evince a very high degree of self-closeness. They evinced but small extent of predisposition to change and a small extent of ability to develop their own regulatory mechanisms to deal with the various problems of social mobilization. Hence they were susceptible to predominance by strongly regulative and restrictive central bureaucratic organizations.

These tendencies both of the broader groups and of the central elite were, as we have seen, in a way only intensified under the impact of the great upsurge of industrialization and urbanization under the aegis of large-scale, bureaucratic agencies and of central control. The speedy tempo of this industrialization and urbanization only tended to intensify the closeness of these groups, the continuous coalescence of regional, status, religious, and occupational division, thus intensifying, in many ways, the cleavages and conflicts among them.

PATTERNS OF ABSORPTION OF CHANGE

The pattern of absorption of change and of protest that has developed in the various split-up regimes evinced quite different characteristics, closely related to the basic modernization orientations of their elites and broader strata and to the specific temporal sequence of modernization that developed within them.

In general in these societies there was a much stronger emphasis on the maintenance of the prevailing social structure. The executive and rather traditional and self-serving bureaucracy predominated, as against the relatively small importance of legislative bodies and parties as arenas of political struggle and decision making, and as bearers of potential political innovations. The bureaucracy and executive tended to deal directly with various interest groups and to look askance on attempts to integrate such interest groups into any wider, active party political frameworks; they attempted to suppress any social movements and more independent public opinion, and employed toward them various repressive measures so as to minimize the possibilities of their developing into active and highly articulated political elements and organizations.

The policies of the rulers aimed mostly at minimizing the potentially disruptive social and political activity of the broader strata. They attempted not to raise the level of political demands, and to anticipate and minimize the possibility of the development of free expression and articulation of such demands. Insofar as any social and economic rights were granted to these strata, they were usually envisaged as gifts from the rulers and not as fully acquired rights. Hence these policies were not successful in effecting symbolic transformation of the center and of developing a new collective political identity or of incorporating new strata in this center.[36]

However, the rulers of these regimes could but rarely have entirely succeeded in their endeavors, and the success of their attempts to minimize all types of change were very often short-lived. Because of their need for some free resources and political support, they usually had to countenance —and often even to foster—some sort of political organizations and some forms of public opinion, even if limited. Hence, the eruptions that tended to develop may have often taken the form not only of mob outbreaks, but also of more organized and articulated forms of political activity and of expression of public opinion. Moreover, the modernizing tendencies and activities of the autocratic elites themselves have often set into motion processes of change beyond their initial intentions.

[36] Neumann, "Germany: Changing Patterns and Lasting Problems," in Neumann, ed., *op. cit.*, pp. 354-94; and A. Gerschenkorn, *Economic Backwardness in Historical Perspective* (Cambridge, Mass.: Harvard University Press, 1962).

ORIENTATIONS OF PROTEST AND PATTERNS OF ERUPTION

As a result of these factors the process of modernization in these countries was set on a course of continual tensions, leading very often to varying attempts of revolutions, although in some cases (especially in Germany) these tensions were partially and temporarily overcome by a successful attempt of the autocratic elite to create, from above, a more differentiated modern political structure, and by the widespread modernizing economic activities of the broader groups.

The structure of the movements of protest in these countries was not seemingly dissimilar to those of western Europe and to some extent the United States.[37] Thus we find here social, political, cultural, and to some extent religious and national movements with similar contents or orientations with regard to some of the basic social, economic, or political problems; and with the similar broad distinction between left and right.[38]

But even on the level of the contents or focuses of protest a very important new characteristic developed, which we shall encounter, in a variety of forms, in many other cases. A tension developed between the attempt to forge out new symbols of national unity and the existing state, which was to some extent the repository of the more traditional symbols of unity.

Unlike in the western European countries, where the early transformation of the political center has minimized such tension, here this split in the sphere of the central symbols and institutions was extremely important.

In close connection with this, despite the similarity of contents, the structural placements as well as the overall significance of their orientations were different. First of all, the temporal coalescence of the different aspects of focuses of protest was greater. Political, socioeconomic, and cultural focuses and symbols of protest tended to coalesce together among different social groups, many of which tended also to develop strong overall negative orientations to the existing regimes. Organizationally they were characterized by their closeness, sectarian orientations, mutual separativeness, and their small degree of susceptibility to becoming integrated in wider political movements or in integrating various interest groups and more independent public opinion.

Hence the dissociation among the different modernizing elites and between them and the broader strata continued to exist in these countries, for relatively long periods. Moreover, as we have seen, with growing social mobilization, urbanization, and partial industrialization and the con-

---

[37] Neumann, *ibid.;* and G. Vernadsky, *A History of Russia* (New Haven: Yale University Press, 1954), Chaps. 12-14.

[38] Kaplan, ed., *op. cit.;* and Neumann, *ibid.*

sequent bringing together of these groups into common institutional frameworks, the possibilities became continually more acute of the development of intensive tensions and strong cleavages between them and of consequent eruptions. The concrete form of such eruptions also depended greatly on the level of differentiation of the social structure, as well as on the extent to which the existing political institutions allow some political organization and expression.

It was in these countries, especially the more developed ones, that the tension between the tendency to mass-consensuality and the split-up in the central institutions and symbols, on the one hand, and the mutual closeness of various elites and strata, on the other, became fully articulated.

The absorptive capacity of these regimes has, therefore, on the whole been a rather limited one, although many of them have successfully maintained themselves for long periods of time. Under the impact of the more violent eruptions they have often become transformed into other types of regimes. Some such changes may have given rise to a type of regime not greatly different from the preceding one. But in some cases new types of regime developed. These were usually some revolutionary regimes, with different new types of orientations to change and with a new, different overall institutional setting.

In the more mixed cases, such as Germany, the combination of national defeat, which undermined the legitimacy of the older order, and of economic expansion, which undermined the validity of the various contractual arrangements, gave rise to the most extreme types of breakdown and attempts of demodernization, of deformation of modernity.[39]

The Process of Modernization in Japan

MODERNIZATION UNDER A REVOLUTIONARY OLIGARCHY

The process of modernization of Japan is of special interest because, although the push to modernization came in Japan under the impact of external forces, i.e., under the impact of Western expansion, yet it has been the only nonwestern European country and "latecomer" that did not evince the basic characteristics of split-up modernization.

It is in comparison with such cases, in which the central political institutions, usually represented by an autocracy, tended greatly to limit the processes of transformation of the social, political, and even economic

[39] Venturi, op. cit.; L. B. Namier, 1848: The Revolution of the Intellectuals (Garden City, N.Y.: Doubleday Anchor Books, 1964); A. Yarmolinski, The Road to Revolution (New York: The Macmillan Company, 1959); and Neumann, "The German Political System," in Beer and Ulam, eds., op. cit., pp. 468-596.

structure, that the uniqueness of Japan stands out.[40] This uniqueness is underlined by the fact that Japan's was possibly the only instance of modernization initiated by an autocratic oligarchy—the Meiji oligarchs, who overthrew in 1868 the Togukawa regime—that was still able to direct and control the course of modernization for a relatively long time, absorbing many new social forces within the frameworks it established. This particular characteristic may perhaps be explained by the fact that this oligarchy was, unlike those of central and eastern Europe, in itself a revolutionary modernizing one, derived from the relatively autonomous tradition of Japanese feudalism which became frozen in the Togukawa regime, strongly committed to modernization of political, administrative, and economic fields, but at the same time basing itself on revival of traditional Imperial symbols.[41]

This continuity of the Imperial tradition was not purely symbolic, but it served as the major focus and content of the new national identity. However, this new identity was couched mostly in terms of particularistic loyalty to the Emperor as Son of Heaven, rather than in terms of his representation of any wider (transcendental) or universalistic orientation.

But while the Meiji oligarchs fostered these traditional symbols they overthrew the older (Togukawa) political system in which the Emperor was a mere figurehead; and they were successful in developing, within the new political system, more flexible central institutions and collective goals. Moreover this elite, while strongly emphasizing innovation in the political field and most adept in political and administrative activity, was also very much oriented to the other social spheres, especially in education and economic activities.[42] By virtue of these characteristics, and because of the fact that it could rely to some extent on support from the wider social groups (such as some of the urban and peasant groups), it could channel (albeit after rather strong initial coercive measures) some of the traditional (feudal and national) loyalties of the wide strata, and through bureaucratic means draw these strata into the new central framework without really granting them, at least at first, full effective political rights. It was only later, when many new groups and strata developed, that the system was faced with very difficult problems of adaptation and absorption.

Perhaps one of the most interesting aspects of the modernization of

[40] H. Norman, *Japan's Emergence as a Modern State* (New York: Institute of Pacific Relations, 1940); A. M. Craig, *Choshu in the Meiji Restoration* (Cambridge, Mass.: Harvard University Press, 1961); R. N. Bellah, *Tokugawa Religion* (New York: Free Press of Glencoe, Inc., 1956); and R. N. Bellah, "Values and Social Change in Modern Japan," *Asian Cultural Studies*, No. 3, Studies on the Modernization of Japan, International Christian University, Tokyo (October 1962), pp. 13-57.

[41] R. A. Scalapino, "Japan between Traditionalism and Democracy," in S. Neumann, ed., *Modern Political Parties* (Chicago: University of Chicago Press, 1956); and T. Ishida, *The Pattern of Japanese Political Modernization*, Proceedings of the Association for Asian Studies, Philadelphia, 1963.

[42] Norman, *op. cit.;* and Scalapino, *ibid.*

Japan has been the attitude of the Meiji oligarchy to traditional symbols and bases of status. The Meiji oligarchs, themselves stemming from secondary aristocratic groups of the samurai, did not only abolish the political and economic power of the older aristocracy and of most of the samurai, but also their status symbols and economic (agrarian) bases, often using the renovated traditional Imperial symbols to legitimize these changes. Instead they created new, more flexible and relatively autonomous criteria and orientations and status, and opened up new possibilities of crystallization of status among many social groups and strata, both old and new.

These strata, with the partial exception of some religious and urban groups, did not evince a high degree of initial self-transformation. Yet they did have strong status orientations to the center as well, and relatively strong achievement orientations oriented to the implementation of collective goals. These were successfully utilized by the Meiji oligarchs to regulate the extent and scope of their social mobilization, especially among the peasantry, but to some extent also among the various new urban groups that were continually created under the impact of the rapid program for industrialization undertaken by the oligarchs.

The class problem which developed in Japan [43] with ongoing urbanization and industrialization was, on the face of it, similar to that of the West —new industrial, commercial, professional, and working classes developed here as in the West. And yet despite these formal similarities, the class structure that developed in Japan differed from the Western one in some crucial characteristics. Here on the whole it was the political change instigated by the Meiji oligarchy that formed the pattern of class structure.

The political and industrializing elite did not hold a large part of its property in land and did not have great interest in the protection of agriculture. From the very beginning this class was urban, bureaucratic (non-gentrylike) and very strongly group- and center-oriented. It was from the beginning very highly bureaucratized, both in the government and in the large business corporations, and there were but few of the free, independent entrepreneurs among them. It was very largely based on formal educational criteria.

A similar pattern of bureaucratization developed in the professions— especially in the legal profession, where most members were employed in the state or corporation bureaucracies, and there existed only a few independent lawyers organized in strong corporate, professional bodies.

Within these new groups there did, however, develop a relatively high level of status flexibility. But this relative status flexibility [44] was not bol-

[43] J. C. Pelzel, "Social Stratification in Japanese Urban Economic Life," Doctoral dissertation, Harvard University, 1949; and E. Vogel, *Japan's New Middle Class* (Berkeley, Calif.: University of California Press, 1963).

[44] R. P. Dore, "The Legacy of Tokugawa Education," in M. B. Jansen, ed., *Changing Japanese Attitudes toward Modernization* (Princeton, N.J.: Princeton University Press, 1965), pp. 99-131; and Scalapino, *op. cit.*

stered up by a concomitant autonomous legitimation and self-perception of the various groups. As for the heavy neo-traditionalism of the center, it set many limitations on the ability of various social and intellectual groups to develop such orientations.

TEMPORAL SEQUENCE AND STRUCTURAL CHARACTERISTICS
OF MODERNIZATION

The temporal sequence of modernization in Japan, although not dissimilar from that of England, developed some characteristics of its own. The modernization of the central political framework took place before the onset of economic change and industrialization, and before the development of a high level of political démarches among the various groups and strata.

At the same time the tempo of urbanization and industrialization was much quicker than in England, Scandinavia, or the Netherlands—much more like the German case. This quick tempo of urbanization, as well as the relatively limited self-transforming and modernizing orientations of the broader traditional groups and their strong dependence on the center, can perhaps explain some of the particular structural characteristics of Japanese modernization.

First of all we witness here the concomitant quick development of large-scale bureaucratization in the economic and social sphere, especially in the industrial sector, together with the *persistence* of small-scale semi-traditional units.[45]

Second, in the rural and to some extent also in the urban industrial sector the process of social mobilization was effected in such a way as to assure the commitment of these groups to the new center, but at the same time, through the persistence or reorganization of various traditional-particularistic arrangements (such as the strong hold of family loyalties), it limited the development of new social and political aspirations.[46]

This process was especially evident in the most crucial economic sphere —that of agriculture. The rural sector was already integrated in the first period in the national market and political sectors. At the same time, through excessive taxation and policies of active mobilization, it was made to pay for the initial push to modernization and to provide the necessary manpower both for industrial and military developments and frameworks.[47]

[45] Bellah, "Values and Social Change in Modern Japan," *op. cit.;* Norman, *op. cit.;* and R. P. Dore, *Land Reform in Japan* (New York: Oxford University Press, Inc., 1959).

[46] Bellah, *ibid.;* H. Norman *op. cit.*

[47] H. Norman, *ibid.*

Third, the process of modernization in Japan was characterized by a specific class structure, analyzed above, and by a concomitant combination of universalistic and particularistic criteria in the regulation and channeling of the process of social mobility and mobilization. The universalistic criteria became most operative in the educational system, in the "entrance" stage to full *occupational* levels—especially in the various periods or stages of examinations to schools and universities, which greatly influenced, if not determined, the differential entry into the occupational and labor market. Beyond these stages, on almost all levels of the social and occupational structure, a series of varied particularistic units tended to crystallize—such as school cliques, company and bureaucratic cliques and groups, small labor groups, etc., within which many traditional forms and attitudes persisted and between which there was but little mobility. At the same time, however, the extent of overlapping between such different particularistic units was relatively small and, most important, there were but few ecological crystallizations of such overlapping. In this way such particularistic developments did not impede—they may have even facilitated—certain status flexibility and recrystallization of status groups, mentioned above.[48]

THE POLITICAL PROCESS AND ABSORPTION OF CHANGE

The focuses of political innovation and decision making in Japan were, in the first periods of the Meiji regime, concentrated in the oligarchy and the new bureaucracy. These two dealt with the promulgation of different policies and regulation of various interest groups, with but minimal recourse to formal representative institutions or public opinion. Only later, in the first decades of the twentieth century, did there gradually and intermittently develop new types of social and political organization, such as parliamentary cliques, some partylike organizations, and various labor organizations.[49]

The major policies of the ruling elite and bureaucracy played a most prominent role in the process of modernization of Japan. They were first focused on provision for the establishment of administrative frameworks, through agricultural taxation of the basic financial and manpower resources necessary for economic development and urbanization, and on laying the foundations of national economic and military strength. In the broader social sphere they were oriented to the mobilization and effective control of the continuously socially mobilized strata, through a widespread educational program (based on the heritage of the Togukawa

[48] Vogel, *op. cit.*

[49] R. E. Ward, "Political Modernization and Political Culture in Japan," *World Politics*, 15 (July 1963), 569-96; and J. Masumi, *Parties and Politics in Contemporary Japan* (Berkeley and Los Angeles, Calif.: University of California Press, 1962).

period) and through widespread propagation of national values through universal conscription.

These processes explain some of the basic characteristics of Japanese modernization—such as its very quick development to a mass society with its consensus centered around the traditional Imperial symbols, with a great weakness of those institutional frameworks (like parliament, legal institution, independent parties, or public opinion) which could foster the development of a civil order and which could assure the orderly and continuous broadening of this consensus and of the transformation of its bases.

In the first periods of political modernization of Japan the articulation of demands and the orientation and organization of protest were still mostly couched in traditional terms and patterns of organization. The articulation of political demands in the beginning of the Meiji period was very minimal. The major types of initial protest orientations and movements were aristocratic and peasant rebellions and outbreaks of the traditional types.[50]

Later, with the growing stabilization and extension of the modern framework, there also developed different new types of intellectual as well as political articulation and protest.[51] These usually contained mixtures of modernizing and traditionalistic elements. Most of them, however, were rather limited in their orientations and demands. The changes demanded by them were in the beginning rather limited to various concrete demands, and only gradually did they become transformed into somewhat more general political demands. These became very closely related to the general development of more flexible types of political organization—the first incipients of partylike activities and flexible types of public opinion, which took place especially after World War I.

However, the patterns of cleavage that developed in Japanese society were rather different from those in the West, although very often similar nomenclatures were used. After the initial conflict between the Meiji oligarchs and the older samurai on the one hand and various peasant groups on the other, the major patterns of cleavage developed around access to the major policy-making and power frameworks in the cabinet and in the bureaucracy—between those groups who allied themselves around the army and those with the civilian parties of the cabinet and of the bureaucracy.

Hence also the focuses or issues of the struggle, although often couched in ideological terms derived from the West, centered mainly on the prob-

[50] H. Passin, "The Stratigraphy of Protest in Japan," in M. Kaplan, ed., *The Revolution in World Politics* (New York: John Wiley & Sons, Inc., 1962), pp. 92-101.

[51] H. Passin, *ibid.;* and I. Morris, ed., *Japan, 1931-1945: Problems in Asian Civilizations* (Boston: D. C. Heath & Company, 1963).

lem of access to the political center, on possibilities of political participation, and on the definition and possibilities of redefinition of the national community and its symbols.

THE BREAKDOWN OF THE JAPANESE SYSTEM
IN THE THIRTIES

The major test of the ability of the Japanese system to absorb new developments came in the Twenties, when new groups and elites in the form of more modern and middle classes, professional and intellectual groups, and some workers' organizations developed much more flexible political organizations and attempted to extend the scope of political participation; although still within the framework of the central bureaucratic institution.

The new modern system failed to absorb these new elements and brought on the breakdown of the older oligarchic-bureaucratic system, and gave rise to the militarist regimes of the Thirties. This development was mostly due to the fact that the rulers attempted to stifle any such new demands and forgo any more flexible policies, and attempted to control them through the bureaucratic and military factions under the aegis of Imperial symbols. The initial incorporation of new demands in the early Meiji period was mostly based on the working of such factions. It was not, however, fully institutionalized beyond their interpersonal relation and hence, when there developed a growing dissociation between the different elites within the different bureaucratic settings—the more modern business and intellectual elites, working class leaders on the one hand, and the more traditional bureaucratic-oligarchic and military elites on the other —the system proved incapable of dealing with the new problems and groups.

The policies developed at that period were characterized by strong repressiveness and by continuous oscillation between overall regulation on the one hand and giving in to the demands of various bureaucratic and military cliques on the other.[52]

It was only under the impact of external forces, i.e., defeat in the war, that a new start took place in Japan. Structurally it was characterized by the continuation of some of the former characteristics of combination of universalistic and particularistic criteria and organization. It was, however, based on the one hand on a rural agrarian reform, and on a great upsurge of industrialization and urbanization under the aegis of a more modernized industrial elite on the other.

The changes effected in the central symbolic sphere by the abolition of

---

[52] M. Maruyama, *Thought and Behavior in Modern Japanese Politics*, ed. I. Morris (New York: Oxford University Press, Inc., 1964); T. Ishida, *Japan's Rapid Development and Its Problems*, mimeographed; and Bellah, "Values and Social Change in Modern Japan," *op. cit.*

the divinity of the Emperor and the institution of a new parliamentary constitutional regime went far to strengthening the institutional underpinnings and frameworks of a civil order.

From the economic and social points of view this new impetus to modernization has up to now evinced a relatively great extent of continuity and growth. But at the same time some of the older weaknesses or problems persisted, and new tensions developed. The transformation in the traditional Imperial symbols did not yet provide a strong basis of new political-institutional consensus.

Hence in addition to the usual problems attendant on later stages of industrialization, other problems specific to the Japanese situation also developed, some of them rooted in the characteristics of the former initial periods of Japanese modernization and the lack of development of a flexible, transcendental national orientation. These problems were manifest in the special structure of Japanese political parties, especially in their factionalism, in the relative weakness of public opinion to cut across such different parties and factions, and in the difficulties of forging a consensus around the working of various autonomous political and nonpolitical regulative institutions.

Perhaps the most extreme manifestation of these problems can be found in the new extreme forms of student protest—as evinced especially in the Zengakuren movement, in its extremist, apolitical trend. This has been the most extreme manifestation of the difficulty of wider, more active groups of the population to develop a new modern identity in some way possibly related to the new political framework.[53]

[53] Passin, "The Stratigraphy of Protest in Japan," in Kaplan, ed., *op. cit.;* Vogel, *op. cit.;* Y. S. Matsumoto, *Contemporary Japan* (Philadelphia: American Philosophical Society, 1960).

In the following chapters we shall proceed
to the analysis of those societies or political
regimes whose basic modern institutional
features were shaped mostly at the second
phase of modernization. Each one started, of
course, from some initial point in the first
phase of modernization, but in each the
problems and processes of the second stage
proved to be more pronounced in the
crystallization of a modern center, as well as
in the modernization of the broader social
groups and strata.

This was largely because the center that was
developed in the first stage was almost
always incapable of dealing with the growing
problems of more
intensive mobilization.

All the societies belonged in their initial
stage of modernization to the split-up type.
They all were latecomers to modernization,
in many cases initially peripheries of various
political or cultural modern centers. The
process of modernization initially developed
mostly under the impact of external forces,
and only to a smaller degree through internal
initiative and transformation of their
broader groups and strata.

Moreover, in most of the countries in question a marked discrepancy tended to develop
between the low level of mobilization and
transformation in the economic and
cultural fields, on the one hand, and the high

CHAPTER FIVE

Patterns Developing in the Second Phase
of Modernization

level of mobilization in the ecological and political fields, on the other; although even in the latter fields many traditional forms persisted.

Some of the major problems these societies faced were owing to the necessity of developing almost entirely new centers, under the impact of relatively intensive processes of social mobilization and mobilization of broader strata; very often without concomitant development of internal regulative mechanisms and value transformations among the groups caught up in these processes.

Because of the central importance of the setting up of new centers, in all of these societies there developed a relative primacy of political and power considerations in the entire process of modernization. Similarly, because of the relative traditionality of these societies, their lower level of differentiation, and the relative weakness of the internal modernizing impulses of the broader strata, the policies undertaken by the centers both for fostering social mobilization and for regulating it were of special importance in the structuring of the modernization process. Three major areas of such policies were of special importance: policies in the agrarian field, which were oriented to open up the great reservoirs of manpower and commitments closed up in the traditional settings; policies in the field of industrialization, which aimed at the transformation of the third major area; economy and educational policies, which had to cope with the motivational reorientation of large parts of the population, in themselves not always internally committed to modernization.

We shall deal here with several major types of such societies, each faced with the same basic problems and each solving them in different ways.

One type, best exemplified by most Latin American countries, is characterized by the continuous development of processes of mobilization side by side with relative lack of ability for crystallization of effective new centers.

The other types are those in which the preceding weak or traditional center has been superseded by a revolutionary movement by new, more modern centers. Three types of such revolutions will be distinguished: a communist revolution, which tends then to establish a totalitarian regime; an internal national revolution oriented against an autocratic traditional-oligarchic regime, as in Mexico and Turkey; and the various nationalist revolutions oriented against foreign colonial regimes, which have established the many postcolonial new states of Asia and Africa.

Patterns of Modernization in Latin America

THE INITIAL PATTERN

The initial situation in most of the Latin American countries during the nineteenth century was characterized by the predominance of relatively weak and oligarchic elites concentrated mostly on establishing a formal modern political framework, culturally oriented mainly to metropolitan Europe, and economically based on landownership and some traditional urban professional ground.[1]

On the other hand, the broader groups and strata, composed mostly of Indian population and of some of the very weak Creole or immigrant middle classes, were mostly entirely confined to their own communities. Little orientation or ability toward participation in any wider framework developed among them.

Economically these societies were heavily and asymmetrically connected with Europe and later the United States, providing as the heritage of the old colonial days (which tended to perpetuate itself, although in new ways throughout the nineteenth and twentieth centuries) mostly raw materials for the international markets, and themselves becoming markets for the processed goods of economic metropolises.

Structurally these societies evinced relatively low differentiation in most spheres, and relatively tenuous relations between the central and local institutions. Most of the interlinking channels between them were organized in a relatively traditional bureaucratic and patrimonial way, with little modern or more differentiated types of professional or voluntary associations or independent middle classes.

From the point of view of basic attitudes to change, these regimes were not dissimilar from those authoritarian or semiauthoritarian regimes that developed in central Europe or in the Middle East, described earlier. If anything, these Latin American regimes in the nineteenth century were even less predisposed to any but the most limited technical changes, attempting at the same time to maintain the social and economic status of the oligarchy. For relatively long periods of time in most of these countries there did not develop either a relatively strong executive bent on some modernization, even if limited, and not only on the maintenance of some institutional framework beneficial to the oligarchy; or some cohesive social movements, or on modernizing intellectual groups and parties.

On the whole, these oligarchies did not evince any strong cohesiveness, nor did they develop any strong ideological orientations beyond maintaining themselves in power and continuing their style of life, identifying themselves socially and culturally with various European centers.[2]

Concomitantly only a few very weak social, political, and cultural symbols common to all the various groups of the population developed. The

[1] K. Silvert, *The Conflict Society: Reaction and Revolution in Latin America* (New Orleans: Hauser, 1961); H. Davis, ed., *Government and Politics in Latin America* (New York: The Ronald Press Company, 1958); E. Lieuwen, *Arms and Politics in Latin America* (New York: Frederick A. Praeger, Inc., 1960); and E. de Vries and M. Echavarria, eds., *Social Aspects of Economic Development in Latin America* (Paris: UNESCO, 1963).

[2] Davis, ed., *ibid.;* and Lieuwen, *ibid.*

war of independence from Spain (or Portugal) did not create many such symbols that could interpenetrate the various strata.

The different groups—the oligarchy and the small, weak middle groups, insofar as they were not entirely identical with the oligarchy, and the broader lower groups—continued on the whole to maintain their own separate ways of life, with few common modern symbols or frameworks. Politically active groups were mostly confined to some oligarchic cliques and traditional groups of petitioners or supplicants.[3]

However, especially in the last third of the nineteenth century, certain important characteristics of the movements of protest developed in many Latin American countries that were also of great importance for the future crystallization of political demands and activities.

The various movements of protest were characterized by great discreteness, organization, and intellectual separateness and closeness, with little cohesion, organizational ability, or ideological strength. On the symbolic level they were mostly committed to some general intellectual trends or orientations, like enlightened rationalism or positivism, with little orientation to concrete problems or appeal to the broader groups of the population.

These movements had, initially at least, little capacity to create new effective symbols of common identity, and they were not capable of transforming the orientations or promoting new symbols of common identification of the various groups of society, or providing any new links between such groups. The great predominance in the Latin American labor movement of syndicalist orientations is one of the most important manifestations of this trend.[4]

Side by side with these types of movement there tended also to develop, among the broader, lower, Indian groups, many outbreaks on the pattern of older peasant rebellions, which evinced little political articulation and organization or connection with the urban movements.

STRUCTURAL CHANGES AND STRUCTURAL DUALITY

The situation started to change in at least some Latin American countries in the latter part of the nineteenth century and in the twentieth, mostly under the impact of external forces—of the world-wide economic expansion and the movements of immigration which came to these countries at the end of the nineteenth century, giving rise to growing social mobilization and differentiation.[5]

[3] Lieuwen, *ibid.;* and J. Johnson, *Political Change in Latin America: The Emergence of the Middle Sectors* (Stanford, Calif.: Stanford University Press, 1958).

[4] See R. Alexander, *Organized Labor in Latin America* (New York: Free Press of Glencoe, Inc., 1965).

[5] G. Germani, *Política y Sociedad en una época de transición* (Buenos Aires: Ed. Paidos, 1962).

This trend of growing social mobilization was manifested, in varying degrees in different countries, in growing urbanization, which did not always go hand in hand with parallel industrialization; the growing politization of broader groups and strata; and, especially in the twentieth century, exposure to various media of mass communication.[6] This was connected with a great rate of social change and disorganization, with the consequent development at a very high, probably unprecedented rate of such social problems as delinquency and crime, family disorganization, and vagrancy.

The continuous differentiation and social mobilization of these groups was characterized by some special features which, while not limited to Latin America (similar features have been also discerned, as we have seen, in some European countries and, in a somewhat different way, as we shall see later, in many of the new states) did, because of the weakness of the center and the quicker tempo of modernization, become more fully discerned in Latin American countries.

The ways in which these problems developed and were dealt with in Latin American countries were greatly influenced by some of the preceding structures—by the existence of weak but politically independent centers, and by the internal and mutual closeness of the different groups and strata.

It was at that period that some of the problems specific to the second stage of modernization started to crystallize in various Latin American countries, to become even more pronounced from the Thirties on.

Perhaps the most important of these characteristics was structural duality within the society; i.e., the coexistence, under conditions of continuous social change, of different social sectors, especially of a disorganized traditional one and a similarly unbalanced and unintegrated modern one.[7]

This duality was evident on several different levels. First, older traditional and relatively more modern structures continued to coexist ecologically, with but little connection between them.[8] The duality was characterized second by the transplantation to the centers of modern life—the cities—of groups of uprooted rural immigrants who formed a new type of urban slum, such as the famous *favelas* in Rio de Janeiro or *villas miserias* in Buenos Aires, which continued to grow with the upsurge of urbanization.[9] Third, and perhaps most important, this structural duality was char-

[6] Silvert, *op. cit.;* and Germani, *op. cit.*

[7] O. Janni, "Delema da Burocratizacao no Brasil," Boletim, *Centro Latino Americano de Pesquisas em Cienciais Sociais,* 4, 3 (August 1960), 9-14; and Johnson, *op. cit.*

[8] T. Di Tella, "Tensiones Sociales de los Paises de la Periferrie," *Revista de la Universidad de Buenos Aires,* Vepoca, 6, 1, 49-62; and J. Ahumada, *Hypotheses for the Diagnosis of a Situation of Social Change: The Case of Venezuela* (Caracas: CENDES, 1963).

[9] R. M. Morse, "Latin American Cities: Aspects of Function and Structure," *Comparative Studies in Society and History,* 4, 4 (July 1962), 473-94; and P. Hauser, ed., *Urbanization in Latin America* (Paris: UNESCO, 1961).

acterized in most Latin American countries—with the partial exception of Mexico, where the revolution opened up the closeness of many groups and established new interlinking mechanisms between them—by the continuation of a basic gap between the rural and urban sectors, the center, and by the ineffectiveness of attempts of agrarian reform and the inability to integrate the rural sectors into more modern settings.[10]

This closeness of the rural sector was one of the most significant characteristics of the social mobilization process in these countries, a social mobilization connected with a relatively high degree of closeness of different groups and strata that were drawn into the new modern, more differentiated ecological setting, seemingly acquiring many characteristics of modernization.

The most important aspect of this closeness was the predominance of a purely adaptive attitude to the wider social setting, with little active solidary orientation to it or identification with it. This adaptive orientation could be manifested in two different, seemingly opposing but often coalescing ways. The first, most frequently found among various traditional lower, and sometimes also middle, rural and urban groups, is characterized by a great extent of rigidity in their conception of society in general and of their own place within it in particular. It was often manifested in a very rigid ritual status image, in very minimal development of any aspirations beyond the traditional scope of occupations or of aspirations to new, different types of community political or social participation, leadership, or organization.[11]

These characteristics were largely rooted in some features of the internal structure of these groups—a strong tendency to minimize internal differentiation with relatively severe sanctions against those who may have tended to break up such homogeneity, a great weakness of flexible self-regulatory mechanisms within these groups, and a minimal ability to enter into or deal with more complex internal or external relations.[12]

They had many repercussions on the structure and activities of these groups when they were pushed into new modernized and differentiated urban, industrial, and semi-industrial settings. They resulted in the perpetuation of traditional types of relationship, i.e., of paternalistic arrangements in industrial settings and relations in dealing with officials, politicians, or leaders of the church, the lack of readiness to undertake responsibility or initiative in the new settings, and in general a great passivity and a small range of interests.

Similarly, new occupational and status aspirations were focused on relatively restricted pre-existing types or ranges of occupational and status

[10] T. F. Carroll, "The Land Reform Issue in Latin America," in A. Hirschmann, ed., *Latin American Issues* (New York: Twentieth Century Fund, 1961), pp. 161-201.
[11] Germani, *op. cit.*
[12] *Ibid.*

conceptions and images. The great propensity to academic, professional, and bureaucratic white-collar occupations, as against more technical and business ones, which is so widely spread in many of these countries on *all levels* of the occupational scale, is perhaps the clearest manifestation or indication of these trends.[13]

Second, this adaptive attitude to the wider social setting could be manifested in exaggerated, unlimited openness and flexibility, and in attempts to obtain within this new setting many various benefits, emoluments, and positions without any consideration of actual possibilities or of other groups in the societies. This tendency is best exemplified by some of the more active urbanized groups in Argentina and other Latin American countries.[14]

These two aspects or consequences of structural duality very often coalesced in the political field, where they gave rise to a very high level of politization, of political aspirations couched very much in terms of the existing status system.

This structural duality was reinforced by the development of what has been called by one Latin American sociologist a situation of "internal colonization," in which the relatively modernized but weak and on the whole oligarchic center kept the periphery in a situation of continuous economic and political deprivation and dependence.[15]

These processes, together with some of the problems of these countries in the international economic sphere, tended greatly to influence the nature of class formation within them. This formation was characterized by the heavy preponderance of old types of professional, communal, and bureaucratic categories (as against industrial-entrepreneurial ones), and by their heavy dependence on the state. This dependence was coupled with little ability of the state to control these occupations and their expansion, as the state and its bureaucratic agencies tended to become major distributive agencies of jobs.

This type of class formation also explains to some extent the special characteristics of the intelligentsia in these countries. Although the heavy preponderance of traditional professional occupations provided a natural breeding ground for intellectuals who could potentially become alienated from the existing system, on the whole such active cohesive intelligentsia groups did not develop as in eastern Europe or in many colonial situations. This was probably owing to the capacity of the state bureaucracies to absorb most of these groups, and the pliability of the center to the demands of the students. Although the universities tended to become a

[13] Hauser, ed., *op. cit.*

[14] Germani, *op. cit.*

[15] R. Stavenhagen, "Classes, Colonialism and Acculturation in Mezoamerica," *Studies in Comparative International Development* (Social Sciences Institute, Washington University, St. Louis, Mo., 1965).

natural seat of socio-political unrest, their political activism seemed to dissipate relatively quickly and was only rarely channelized into continuous transformative groups or political activities.

Relatively few groups developed within these societies that evinced somewhat greater flexibility and more realistic orientations. Most important among them were some economic and business communities or new professional groups, some relatively rare noneruptive rural leadership, and some reformative religious groups. But in most of the societies studied here these were weak, and above all relatively segregated both from the central institutions of the societies and from wider social strata. Even though new types of specialized and differentiated social organizations, trade unions, or professional organizations were created both among the elite and among the broader groups of society that were drawn into new frameworks, this did not result in the creation of a viable new differentiated institutional structure.[16]

These groups were unable to function effectively because they had to work under false premises, i.e., some of the prerequisites for their effective functioning did not develop in these settings. They very often exhibited characteristics of what has been called by a student of French "retardation" or "traditionalism," "delinquent communities," [17] i.e., communities not oriented to the attainment of their manifest goals (economic growth, community development, or the like) but to the maintenance of the vested status and interest positions of their members within the existing settings.

Moreover, even though there tended to develop, within some institutional spheres—in education, in the field of economic enterprise, or in the professions—some more stable differentiated groups and organizations, their ability to develop and maintain their organization and activities within the wider setting was very restricted. Very often they succumbed to the pressures of the environment, becoming disorganized or "delinquent," i.e., enclosed in their own interests without being able to orient themselves to wider contacts and frameworks.[18]

ELITE FORMATION AND STRUCTURAL DUALITY

These various manifestations of structural duality and closeness among the broader strata were to no small degree paralleled by certain orientations that developed among the elites, which began to crystallize in the second stage of modernization in many of the Latin American countries.

---

[16] Fernandes, op. cit.

[17] J. R. Pitts, "Continuity and Change in Bourgeois France," In Search of France (Cambridge, Mass.: Harvard University Press, 1963), esp. pp. 254-59.

[18] Pitts, ibid.; and Germani, op. cit.

Two broad types of such elites and orientations can be discerned. One was a continuation of the older oligarchic elite, with some new additions, mainly in the form of military and big business groups.[19] Side by side with these there developed, out of the processes of continuous social mobilization, new more demagogic or populistic elites, recruited both from older conservative-traditional and more modern groups.[20] Both types of elite developed a rather ambivalent attitude to modernization, but the nature of this ambivalence differed greatly between them.

The more traditional oligarchic elites, which persisted in many of the Latin American countries or became closely related to various conservative military cliques and groups, tended to evince a type of attitude to change that was characteristic of the more autocrative regimes in the former period. However, in the condition of growing social mobilization even they had to have greater recourse to various more sophisticated media of control and mass communication and to the use of more modern political and social symbols.[21]

The more modern populistic elites attempted to implement various more variegated modernized policies and to establish more visible common frameworks and symbols. Yet among many of these elites the attitude to change was usually a combination of attempts to find easy ways to establish modern frameworks and to control the mobilized masses without effecting a structural transformation of major parts of the society—with the problem of agrarian reform serving as the Achilles' heel of many attempts at such reform.[22]

These elites tended to develop a whole range of more dynamic policies —which, however, paradoxically enough often tended only to reinforce the structural duality of the societies.

The most important common denominator of these policies has been the continuous oscillation between attempts of the ruling elites at controlling all the major power positions and groups in the society and monopolizing the positions of effective control, and a continuous giving in to the demands of various groups. Examples of such oscillating policies could be found in many important fields.

Thus, first, in almost all these countries there took place a continuous expansion and swelling of the bureaucracies by new aspirants, and a continual giving in by the rulers to the growing demands of the holders of these positions for tenure of office and for increased (even if not fully

[19] Silvert, *op. cit.;* and Johnson, *op. cit.*

[20] K. Silvert, *A Note on Chile and Argentina,* American Universities Field Staff Report Service, 8, 8 (1961).

[21] Ahumada, *op. cit.*

[22] De Vries and Echavarria, eds., *op. cit.;* and C. Furtado, *A Pre-Revolucao Brasileira* (Rio de Janeiro: Editora Fundo de Cultura, 1962).

adequate to catch up with the growing inflation) wages and emoluments.[23]

A similar oscillation can be found in the field of agrarian reform.[24] In many of these countries very far-reaching official programs of redistribution of land were attempted. These programs often resulted in disorganization of the agricultural traditional rural setting, and in the resistance of various vested interests that attempted to utilize the situation for their own self-aggrandizement. Vested interests that tended to obstruct attempts at the modernization of agriculture could be upheld both by landlords and by the new peasant proprietors. Both often succeeded in evading and subverting the policies of the government aimed at increase of technical output, modernization of agriculture, etc.

In many cases the agencies of rural improvement—credit agencies, community development centers established by the government—were taken up and swallowed, as it were, by these vested interests, against the goals and policies of the government, without the government being able to control them effectively.[25]

In the field of education the rulers oscillated between attempting to repress autonomous activities of the students and direct them in their educational activities, on the one hand, and giving in to their demands on the other. As a result, one of the most important developments in the field was the very quick swelling of numbers of students in various educational institutions—especially in humanistic, academic high schools and in the more traditional (humanistic, legal) faculties of the universities. Similarly, the rulers tended to give in to the demands of students and in educational and pedagogical fields there was a consequent lowering of standards. Very often side by side with this there took place many rather unsuccessful attempts by the rulers to control the students—attempts to direct them to the nonacademic (technical, professional) subjects and to maintain some discipline among them.[26]

In the sphere of economic policy proper, the examples of regimentation and confiscation which lowered the efficiency of the economic sectors on the one hand, and of wide redistributive measure to various parts of the population on the other, are too numerous and well known to require any detailed illustration.[27]

In implementing these policies the new rulers not only succumbed to pressures from different groups, but very often themselves created and legitimized such pressures. Thus a very general result of these policies was

[23] De Vries and Echavarria, eds., *ibid.;* and SUR, *Argentina, 1930-1960* (Buenos Aires, 1961).

[24] Carroll, *op. cit.;* and Hauser, ed., *op. cit.*

[25] *Ibid.*

[26] S. M. Lipset, "University Students and Politics in Underdeveloped Countries," *Minerva,* Vol. 3, No. 1, Autumn 1964, pp. 15-56.

[27] *Ibid.;* and de Vries and Echavarria, eds., *op cit.*

to reduce available resources and to squander them. Such squandering of resources took place often for symbolic or ideological reasons, and because of the search of the rulers for support and their attempts to attest in this way to their legitimation. It usually minimized the range of maneuvering ability available to these elites. At the same time, because of lack of any clear principles of regulation or priorities, they tended to exacerbate the level of conflict between various groups as the aspiration of them all rose, while the total output of the economy remained static or even decreased.

Thus extremely important parallels developed in the orientations and activities of the new elites and of large parts of the broader groups and strata. Both were characterized by development, within the new modern institutional frameworks, of relatively rigid and restricted social, cultural, and political orientations. In both cases these orientations and aspirations were largely conceived either in terms of some of the status and symbols derived mostly from the preceding social structure and focused in a relatively rigid way on some possibilities within these structures, or in terms of flexible but unattainable goods.[28]

These parallel developments in the orientations of the elites and of the broader groups and strata go far to explain the continually recrystallized structural duality that tended greatly to impede the development of more self-modernizing and effective groups, while at the same time they tended also—especially through continuous inflation which developed under the pressure of varied economic and political trends—to undermine the modern economic frameworks.

The various processes analyzed above may explain some of the major characteristics of Latin American development as a mass society. As in Japan, there developed here a very intensive tendency to mass society, but unlike in Japan these tendencies did not have a strong traditional focus of consensus. From the very beginning it was in these basic focuses or symbols of common identity that these countries were weak, and these weaknesses, as well as the various manifestations of structural duality, undermined the effective functioning of those institutions—parliaments, associations, public opinion—that could serve as frameworks of development of a civil order.

There also developed a discrepancy between the existing state organization and nationalist movements, but of a somewhat different kind from what we saw in various eastern European countries. It was not that the existing state was seen as an obstacle to new nationalism or its enemy, but rather that there were but few cases in which new, effective, binding symbols of nationalism were forged out that could be infused, as it were, into the existing political center or even oppose them effectively.

[28] Germani, *op. cit.;* and Ahumada, *op. cit.*

STRUCTURAL DUALITY AND BREAKDOWNS

Whatever the differences between them, the different Latin American countries—with the exception of Mexico, which will be analyzed later on —evinced some specific characteristics, the most important of which was the weakness of the new centers, which became crystallized in the second stage of modernization.

This was most manifest in the relative weakness of common symbols of national identity and of common, acceptable rules of the political game, and in the relative lack of cohesiveness and of the ruling elites.

All this can perhaps be seen most clearly in the continual oscillation of the ruling elites in their policies with regard to far-ranging structural (especially agrarian) reforms and the consequent development—especially within the more modernized and differentiated societies—of many manifestations of breakdowns and regressions, after what might have been seen as take-off into modernity.

The most striking illustration of such development can be found in Argentina, where after the initial great economic upsurge and the attempts to establish a constitutional regime in the first two to three decades of the twentieth century there developed intermittent economic regressions and, in the political field, the Peronist regime and the continuous post-Peronist vicissitudes and instability.[29]

Similarly, a continuous economic and political lack of stability can be found in other Latin American countries, where there often develops a succession of new political regimes, be they military dictatorships or combinations of various oligarchic and populist groups unable to cope continuously and effectively with many of the problems of modernization.[30]

But this very combination of continuous social mobilization, together with the manifestation of structural duality, the oscillation of the elites, and the continuous political and economic instability, gave rise to new, more active and articulated movements of protest and to a constant search for new common symbols and attempts to create more cohesive central frameworks.

The most important characteristic of these new patterns of political organization was a continual oscillation between violent outbursts, separatist activities, and orientations in the tradition of the older period and the development of a tendency toward the development of mass parties with strong totalistic orientations. Such parties often attempted to organize, within the context of one party, both distinct, separate groups and more general, diffuse movements and orientations, which could effec-

---

[29] G. Pendle, *Argentina* (3rd ed.) (New York: Oxford University Press, Inc., 1963); and SUR, *op. cit.*

[30] Lieuwen, *op. cit.*

tively mobilize wider masses. They also tended to develop new symbols of protest in which national, social, and populistic symbols often tended to become combined together in new types of parties.

These developments have recently been summarized by DiTella in describing the rise of what he calls monolithic ideologies in competitive party systems in Latin America:

Typical of Latin America is a coalition of monolithically oriented elites plus massified working class (urban or rural) that has been called by Gino Germani *"nacionalismo popular."* It includes several varieties, and ranges from *fidelismo* to *peronismo,* including the *aprista* type parties. This peculiar type of coalition —not uncommon in underdeveloped countries—tends to be very powerful in electoral terms, and to govern monolithically when it holds power, particularly in the early stages of its consolidation as such a *"nacionalista popular* coalition."* But, while a threat to democracy, it is at the same time the most likely cement with which to build one of the foundations of democracy; an opposition with the capacity to oppose.

Under conditions of a more stabilized economic development, or after war-induced tensions have disappeared, the coalition tends to break up due to the absorption of its non-working class elites into the mass of the middle and upper middle classes. In these cases there is evidence that many of the working class supporters remain in the *"nacionalista popular"* movement, though losing some marginal supporters. The monolithic ideology generally remains, though expressed in a more moderate form, and performs the function of maintaining the organizational strength of the *"nacionalista popular"* party. Being thus one of the bases for the continuance of a strong opposition to the conservative establishment, it may be hypothesized that the monolithic ideology is functional to the establishment of competitive party system, at this period of development of the Latin American political system.[31]

In these movements we find some interesting transformation or change of the usual nomenclature of political protest. Perhaps the most outstanding characteristic of the movement of protest as they tended to develop in Latin American countries was the special mixture between socio-economic and political motives and focuses. If the socio-economic structure tended to engender the usual (i.e., the European) division between left and right, with a strong agrarian motive on the left, the development of the new demagogic elites, which were oriented to the wider strata without effecting any far-reaching structural changes, created a situation in which political-populistic themes were often borne by economically conservative or at least nontransformative groups. Hence, the usual distinction between left and right often tended to lose its accepted meaning, because many of the popular lower-class movements were oriented not only to the acquisition of new social and economic benefits, but also to

[31] T. S. Di Tella, "Monolithic Ideologies in Competitive Party Systems: The Latin American Case," *Transactions of the Fifth World Congress of Sociology,* 3 (1962), 181-90.

the establishment of new common symbols of national identification, which was often couched in extreme nationalistic terms, often tending to assume more totalistic and divisive characteristics.

Side by side with these new types of political organization, sometimes in alliance with them and sometimes in opposition, there also developed new attempts to develop some new interlinking mechanisms and to create new, more flexible symbols and focuses of national identity.

These new, more flexible orientations and the concomitant attempts at the establishment of more viable new central frameworks were developed mainly by those new groups and elites such as professional, entrepreneurial, or intellectual groups which attempted to overcome the closeness of the major groups and strata through far-reaching structural reforms—whether in the field of agrarian reform or new educational policies —and to establish new business enterprises based on more professional managerial orientations.

These groups were also, to use Hirschman's term, the main "reform-mongers" who attempted to implement these varied reforms through a variety of coalitions with both the older, more oligarchic elites and the more populist-demagogic ones.[32]

These attempts at structural reform, on the one hand, and the varied new types of political organization described above on the other, were strongly connected with a constant search for some new central symbols and for the recrystallization of central institution. This search has been going on in almost all Latin American countries, but in different forms and directions.

DIFFERENCES AMONG LATIN AMERICAN COUNTRIES

The major differences between various Latin American countries were influenced first by the extent of their modernization, of the breakdown of the traditional settings, second by the tempo of social mobilization, and last by the development of some viable new common frameworks and symbols.

At the most modern extreme we find Argentina.[33] Throughout the last three decades of the nineteenth century and the first two of the twentieth there developed, through continuous immigration and colonization, different new, relatively modern, groups, such as industrial entrepreneurs, planters, workers, etc. These groups tended, on the whole, to be rather separate socially and culturally. However, because of the continuous economic expansion and colonization in an open frontier line set-up they were able to maintain their separate existence and mutual

[32] *Ibid.*

[33] A. Hirschman, *Journeys towards Progress: Studies of Economic Policy Making in Latin America* (New York: Twentieth Century Fund, 1963).

closeness together with continuous development, change, and modernization. They became interwoven only gradually into a closer framework of mutual interdependence. At the same time, the major oligarchic elites which held the ruling positions in the country did not develop new symbols, institutions, and policies capable of dealing with these new problems, and socially maintained the framework developed in the mid-nineteenth century, thus impeding the full integration of these groups into new, more modern frameworks.

It was only when the interrelation between these groups became close and the continued economic expansion became halted that the shaky coexistence was broken down, giving rise to long periods of conflicts and tension in the thirties, then to the Peronist regime, and later continuing some of the same institutional instabilities.

At the other extreme we find such traditional oligarchic-military regimes as Paraguay,[34] only now beginning to undergo the first steps to more far-reaching modernization.

Between these two extreme types we find a great variety of regimes, differing in the degree of their flexibility and ability to deal with problems of modernization—in their continuous cases of breakdowns and possible transformations. Of special interest in this context are the situations that developed in Brazil, Venezuela, and Chile.[35] In different ways these three countries evince the most extreme manifestations of structural duality and relatively weak centers. Thus, the tempo of urbanization and social mobilization has been relatively quick in these countries—as is also the extent of social disorganization and the transplantation of such disorganized structures into modern settings. At the same time (especially in Brazil) large reservoirs of traditional communities and attitudes existed. These communities and attitudes often became very important impediments to the process of modernization, and tended to reinforce the crystallization of structural duality. At the same time, however, they could also, as in Mexico, provide relatively important focuses or starting points for the development of new national identity.

The search for ways to overcome this structural duality and to develop new types of national identity goes on in the Latin American countries in a variety of different ways. In some countries, especially Chile and Venezuela, attempts have developed lately to overcome the divisive outcomes of structural duality, political violence, and oscillatory policies through the democratic process, aiming at the establishment of a strong center capable of developing a new consensus around far-reaching structural reforms.[36]

[34] G. Pendle, *Paraguay: A Riverside Nation* (New York: Oxford University Press, Inc., 1963).

[35] Davis, ed., *op. cit.;* Lieuwen, *op. cit.;* and Ahumada, *op. cit.*

[36] Ahumada, *op. cit.;* and Janni, *op. cit.*

Within this context the case of Bolivia is of special interest,[37] where an internal national revolution took place based ˋon a pattern similar to the earlier Mexican one, but until now it was not able to evince any cohesiveness among its component groups of ability to a new center and seems to have disintegrated, reverting, perhaps only temporarily, to a semimilitary autocracy.

At the other extreme we find the extremely revolutionary movement, most clearly illustrated by Castro's Cuba, which attempts to create new centers through an overall overthrow of the preceding regime to establish an entirely new, presumably populist communist regime.[38]

These various types of attempts and movements to create new viable centers can be found, in varying degrees, in all Latin American countries, and the future of Latin America will depend to no small degree on the relative strength of these movements in relation to the forces of inertia, on the one hand, and on their strength in relation to one another, on the other.

Revolutionary-nationalist and Communist Regimes

COMMON CHARACTERISTICS OF THE REVOLUTIONARY REGIMES

We shall proceed now to the analysis of some of the major types of revolutionary regime that developed out of the breakdown of the more autocratic regimes in situations of split-up modernization, and which created new relatively effective modern centers, within which there developed new orientations to change. We shall deal first with those regimes which developed mostly through an internal revolution, i.e., a revolution directed against autochthonous, ruling autocracy.

As has been indicated above, two major types of such regimes can be distinguished. One, best seen in Turkey [39] and Mexico,[40] can be called a

---

[37] C. A. M. Hennessy, "Shifting Forces in the Bolivia Revolution," *World Today*, **20,** 5 (August 1964), 197-207.

[38] W. MacGetty and C. R. Banet, eds., *Twentieth-Century Cuba: The Background of the Castro Revolution* (Garden City, N.Y.: Doubleday Anchor Books, 1965); and D. Seers *et al., Cuba: The Economic and Social Revolution* (Chapel Hill, N.C.: University of North Carolina Press, 1964).

[39] K. Karpat, *Turkey's Politics: The Transition to a Multi-Party System* (Princeton, N.J.: Princeton University Press, 1959); B. Lewis, *The Emergence of Modern Turkey* (London: Oxford University Press, 1961); K. Karpat, "Recent Political Developments in Turkey and Their Social Background," *International Affairs*, **28,** 3 (July 1962), 304-23; and F. W. Frey, "Political Development, Power and Communications in Turkey," in L. W. Pye, ed., *Communication and Political Development* (Princeton, N.J.: Princeton University Press, 1963).

[40] H. F. Cline, *Mexico: Revolution to Evolution* (London: Oxford University Press, 1962); R. E. Scott, *Mexican Government in Transition* (Urbana, Ill.: University of Illinois Press, 1959); O. Paz, *The Labyrinth of Solitude: Life and Thought in Mexico*

national revolution, where the symbols of the new regimes were couched mostly in terms of national and popular orientation, the purely social or socialist playing mostly a secondary role.

The second type of such revolutionary regimes emphasized mainly social orientations of protest as bases for new symbols. The most significant of these, of course, has been the communist regime in Russia [41] and later in China.[42]

The major differences between these countries and the various developments in Latin America analyzed above has been that here relatively cohesive elites oriented to modernization developed which were able to crystallize some type of a new more efficient and flexible modern center.

Both types of such revolutionary regimes developed from relatively similar backgrounds—from situations of split-up modernization in which oligarchic or autocratic regimes, often after defeat in war, had lost the ability to control the process of modernization in their societies. But beyond this major differences developed in the nature of the elite groups that became most predominant after the breakdown of the preceding regimes.

In the case of the national revolution these were groups with strong internal orientations and relatively weaker international ones. They were usually composed of a combination of intellectual, bureaucratic, professional, and/or military groups not entirely alienated from the pre-existing elites, and some of the broader groups of the society and groups that held elite positions in the preceding structure, and had somewhat closer relations with the broader social strata.[43]

In the communist case the predominant elites were more oriented to international settings, more alienated both from the preceding social

---

(New York: Grove Press, 1961), esp. Chaps. 6-8; and R. Vernon, *The Dilemma of Mexico's Development: The Roles of the Private Sectors* (Cambridge, Mass.: Harvard University Press, 1963).

[41] M. Fainsod, *How Russia Is Ruled* (Cambridge, Mass.: Harvard University Press, 1955); Z. K. Brzezinski, *Ideology and Power in Soviet Politics* (New York: Frederick A. Praeger, Inc., 1962); J. A. Armstrong, *The Politics of Totalitarianism: The Communist Party of the Soviet Union from 1934 to the Present* (New York: Random House, Inc., 1961); and R. A. Feldmesser, "Social Class and Political Structure," in C. E. Black, ed., *The Transformation of Russian Society* (Cambridge, Mass.: Harvard University Press, 1960), pp. 235-53.

[42] F. Schurman, *Ideology and Organization in Communist China* (Berkeley, Calif.: University of California Press, 1966); and F. Michael, "The Role of Law in Traditional, Nationalist and Communist China," *The China Quarterly*, 9 (January–March 1962), 124-48.

[43] S. N. Eisenstadt, "Bureaucracy and Political Development," in J. La Polambara ed., *Bureaucracy and Political Development* (Princeton, N.J.: Princeton University Press, 1963), pp. 96-120; E. Shils, "Demagogues and Cadres in the Political Development of New States," in Pye, ed., *op. cit.*, pp. 64-78; and M. Janovitz, *The Military in the Political Development of New Nations* (Chicago: University of Chicago Press, 1964).

structure and, at least initially, from the broader strata of their societies as well.[44]

In a way it is a moot question to what extent the predominance of any such elite in a given society was preordained, and to what extent it was due to accident and vicissitudes of the play of different social forces. The available historical evidence seems to lead to the conclusion that any such development was not necessarily preordained, and was to no small extent influenced by such vicissitudes.

But once any such elite became predominant and evinced a relatively high degree of cohesiveness, it could impose its own type of institutional patterns and of orientation to change, which of course differed greatly between these two types of regime.

Despite the obvious differences between these two types of revolutionary regime some similarities also exist between them; especially in the problems they faced, rooted as they were in some similar situations. They all aimed to attain structural and ideological transformation, both on the level of the central institutions and of the broader strata.[45]

On the central level the leaders of these new regimes attempted to establish a new institutional order with its own new symbols of the center. These were forged out of the basic orientations of protest from which these revolutions crystallized, and combined—in different emphasis, as we have seen—nationalistic-cultural and social themes.

Similarly, both types of regime effected important transformations in the central symbolic and political spheres, attempting to incorporate various local-ethnic elements to transcend those older elements—such as Islam in Turkey, the Spanish-colonial in Mexico, or Marxist and Russian Orthodox in Russia—which seemed to the leaders to be divisive and not able to provide a common new modern focus of identification. They also overcame, in different degrees, the tension between the state and nationalism that existed in these societies in the previous stages, making the new political frameworks into focuses of the new national identity.

Parallel to this they aimed to loosen up the older traditional settings and to effect some transformation attitudes and orientations of the broader strata, to open them up toward the new center and to push them in the direction of growing social, cultural, and economic differentiation and mobilization.[46]

Within this context problems of agrarian reform and transformation

[44] V. C. Nahirny, "The Russian Intelligentsia: From Men of Ideas to Men of Convictions," *Comparative Studies in Society and History*, 4, 4 (July 1962), 403-35; and F. Venturi, *Roots of Revolution* (New York: Alfred A. Knopf, Inc., 1960).

[45] E. Shils, *Political Development in the New States* (The Hague: Mouton, 1962); and J. N. Kautsky, ed., *Political Change in Underdeveloped Countries: Nationalism and Communism* (New York: John Wiley & Sons, Inc., 1962).

[46] Pye, ed., *op. cit.*, esp. chaps. by E. Shils, F. W. Frey, H. Hyman, and D. Lerner.

became of crucial importance. The transformation of the agrarian scene opened up the great reservoirs of manpower, and of potential identification with new national symbols that until then were closed up in traditional settings and served as an important stumbling block on the road to modernization.

In general the most crucial aspect of these attempts of the elites at structural transformation of their societies was the establishment of certain interlinking and integrative mechanisms between the local and central levels. Most of these mechanisms were organized, at least initially, in party and bureaucratic and political organizations. It was through these frameworks that the ruling elites attempted to draw these groups into the more differentiated institutional framework, and at the same time to regulate, at least to some extent, their integration within it, and to impose their own policies on them. In this they greatly differed from the more oscillating elites we have encountered in many of the Latin American countries.

This could be seen in the details of the policies these elites developed to deal with problems of modernization. Thus, for instance, the restructuring of the process of communication [47] was effected in these countries by gradual linking of different levels and their gradual incorporation into a relatively unified system. An important aspect of this process was that for a period of time the different levels or types of communicative patterns were kept relatively segregated, while special interlinking mechanisms which maintained some relation to the central communicative system by the elites were gradually but steadily expanded.

These elites were relatively more flexible in their status orientations and at the same time more firm in the implementation of their policies.[48] They did not give in indiscriminately to the demands of different groups and strata within their societies. In extreme cases, as in Russia, the elites used coercion against these groups, but in others they attempted rather to direct, manipulate, and regulate their demands.

The same picture could also be seen in the field of educational policies.[49] Thus, in most of these countries a widespread extension of primary education developed on the local level, side by side with the extension of special new secularized and diversified elite schools, with only a gradual extension of mobility between these levels.

Third, and perhaps most important from the point of view of our discussion, has been the structuring of the processes of social mobility

[47] *Ibid.;* and S. N. Eisenstadt, "Communication Systems and Social Structure; An Exploratory Comparative Study," *Public Opinion Quarterly,* **19** (Summer 1955), 153-57.

[48] Nahirny, *op. cit.;* Venturi, *op. cit.;* and A. Yarmolinski, *The Road to Revolution* (New York: The Macmillan Company, 1959).

[49] S. N. Eisenstadt, *Education and Political Development,* Duke University Commonwealth Seminar Series (Durham, N.C.: Duke University Press, 1962-63).

in these societies.[50] In all these countries processes of mobility developed that inevitably broke down the self-sufficiency of at least some of the traditional units and brought them into the framework of the new, more modernized institutions. This mobility was on the whole geared to realistic expanding opportunities—at least, the discrepancy between the mobility aspirations and the realities of expanding economies was not as great as in the other cases, especially Latin America and many new states.

The processes of mobility were closely connected with the development of some new, more differentiated status and occupational orientations and aspirations and a growing internal differentiation within the local rural or urban units. They gave rise to some important changes in the structure of leadership and community participation, and to growing connections between these groups and the central institutions.

In all these countries the new rulers were obviously greatly interested in maintaining monopoly of power and allocation of status, but they attempted to develop and maintain such monopoly together with a growing variegation of the symbols and frameworks of status. They also stressed the importance of political status, but usually attempted to connect it with emphasis on new occupational, technical, and professional activities. They also attempted to minimize, as far as possible, various tendencies to ascriptive monopolization of upper positions by various elite and bureaucratic groups.

These policies were able to overcome or minimize, at least initially, some of the characteristics and consequences of structural duality that were incipient in these societies.

But these elites constantly faced two difficult problems, separated but often related. One was rooted in the relative conservativeness and closeness of many of the more traditional groups, especially of the peasantry—a closeness which could become easily transferred, as in Latin America, into the urban setting as well. The second problem was due to the possibility that more modernized, differentiated groups would develop, with more intensive demands which would go beyond the limits initially set up by the elites.

STRUCTURAL CHARACTERISTICS OF
NATIONALISTIC-REVOLUTIONARY REGIMES

Beyond these common characteristics, of course, several crucial differences developed between those two types of revolutionary regimes. Let

[50] Eisenstadt, *ibid.*; C. N. Myers, *Education and National Development in Mexico* (Princeton, N.J.: Princeton University Press, 1965); and E. A. Tiryakian, "Occupational Stratification and Aspiration in an Underdeveloped Country: The Philippines," *Economic Development and Cultural Change*, 7 (1959), 431-44.

us start first with the nationalistic types of revolution, exemplified by the Mexican and Turkish cases.

While the leaders of these revolutions aimed at long-range structural transformation in the society, they did not envisage this transformation as a total reshaping of the social structure. They also attempted to take into account some of the major social groups and strata, or at least to permit them some autonomous expression, at the same time attempting to regulate such new demands. They tended to develop relatively positive orientations to the orientations and aspirations of different groups, and especially to emphasize new common, i.e., mostly national, symbols, which would be binding on all of them.[51]

In the ideological and value spheres the leaders of those revolutions aimed at the development of a new, more flexible set of symbols and collective identity which, while not negating the traditions of various parts of the society, would also provide some meaning for the new processes of change.

On the structural-institutional level these regimes attempted to establish widespread monolithic executives, dominant parties, and/or central bureaucratic organizations, into which various trade union and professional organizations also became integrated, and through which the demands of various groups were regulated and absorbed.

Some of these demands, such as those for agrarian reform in Mexico, have become important symbols of the new regime; but their economic policies were usually a combination of "étatism" with some encouragement of private and semipublic developments.

In finance and industry—the key new economic sectors—they tended to emphasize heavily, though not exclusively, the public, governmental sector, while at the same time they permitted parallel controlled developments in the private sector. Accordingly the class formation that developed leaned heavily toward the more bureaucratic types of occupational channels.

Interestingly enough, the actual policies related to these symbols did not always fully implement all the potential demands that could, and very often did, develop in connection with their symbols. Thus, for instance, agrarian reforms implemented in Mexico were important from the point of view of the restructuring of internal arrangements of the rural communities, creating new social and economic groups within them and opening up new channels of mobility to the center. But on the whole these reforms were not allowed to block the expansion of the economy, through giving in to both old and new vested interests.[52]

[51] See footnote 1; also, Lewis, *op. cit.*; Karpat, "Recent Political Developments in Turkey," *op. cit.*; and Cline, *op. cit.*

[52] J. G. Maddox, *Mexican Land Reform*, American Universities Field Staff, JGM–5–57 (New York, 1957).

The party, and/or the executive, served as the main focuses of political decision making and political innovation. Parties were the main focuses of impetus to change, of the formulation of various policies aimed at cliques, and of mobilization of support of new policies. At the same time, however, these parties did not aim at a close and monolithic integration of all the various groups and movements and independent public opinion, nor at the total negation of their autonomous political expression. Usually they allowed, willingly or unwillingly, some such expression. Gradually there even developed some recourse within them to the legislative and the executive as media of political discourse, innovation, and decision making, and to the bureaucracy as an important, to some extent autonomous, instrument of implementation and execution of such policies.

In later stages of development these characteristics enabled a growing shift to bureaucracy and even to the legislature as the more important media of political decision.[53]

GROWING DIFFERENTIATION AND NEW ORIENTATIONS
OF PROTEST

With the institutionalization of the political order of these regimes, and with the growing differentiation of the social structure and growing social mobilization, there developed new demands for political participation and new orientations and organizations of protest.

The major problems and orientations of protest that tended to develop stemmed either from lack of integration of the varied groups into the new center, or from the attempts of other, more active groups to transform it into some new, often more flexible, direction. The first type of problem could develop mainly from within the more traditional groups, like the peasant and orthodox Muslim circles in Turkey, which wanted to utilize the greater flexibility of the new setting for the implementation of the more traditional settings and goals.[54]

The second type of problem of demand tended to develop especially from within more modern and flexible groups, like professional, middle-class, and workers' organizations and intellectual groups. These groups tended to develop new demands to the extension of participation in the political process, and for more flexible policies.

The problems of the integration of these varied groups usually became more acute with steady onset of modernization and industrialization and with the development of greater structural differentiation, of more autonomous orientations and demands, and of growing mobility. These

[53] Cline, op. cit.; Lewis, op. cit.; and Karpat, "Recent Political Developments in Turkey," op. cit.

[54] Karpat, ibid.; Karpat, Turkey's Politics; and Frey, op. cit.

developments inevitably tended to increase and intensify conflict between different sectors, urban and rural, modern and traditional; within
any such sector; between different elite groups; and between them and
older elites.

The orientations of protest and the eruptions that tended to develop
often took the form of uprisings and rebellions as well as of the more
differentiated orientations and organizations, these two types often coalescing together.

The special problem or difficulty that many of the protest movements
encountered was that the revolutionary regimes against which their activities were oriented had already preempted many of the possible symbols of protest, and hence they had some difficulty in forging wider
ideological orientation and organizational frameworks. Hence also the
older symbols of "right" and "left" often lost their overall meaning. The
extent of the ability of these regimes to deal with the development of
such new orientations and organizations of protest varied. Mexico has,
up to now, evinced a great ability to absorb most such new forms within
the framework of its dominant party regime. This was done by a series
of policies that assured relatively steady economic growth and were
flexible enough to accede to some of the new demands, and by a reorganization of the party in such a way that it became a much more
differentiated and flexible organization that could accommodate new
interests and groups.[55]

In Turkey,[56] on the other hand, the new multiparty regime that was
established after World War II was not able, at least at first, to accommodate the new forces in a viable structure. This weakness led to
partial breakdowns and to military coups that attempted to restore the
constitutional regime, which is still struggling to assure its basic acceptance and continuity.

SPECIFIC CHARACTERISTICS OF THE COMMUNIST REGIMES

The revolutionary elites of these regions were very cohesive and power
oriented, and in their basic social and political orientations they were
much more alienated from the pre-existing structure, and from the broader
groups and strata. In many respects they evinced the basic characteristics
of closed sects with very strong totalistic ideological orientations, on the
one hand, and coercive attitudes to broader strata of the population on
the other.[57]

This could be seen first in the nature of symbolic transformations that

[55] Cline, *op. cit.*; Scott, *op. cit.*; Paz, *op. cit.*; and Vernon, *op. cit.*
[56] Karpat, *Turkey's Politics;* Lewis, *op. cit.*; Karpat, "Recent Political Developments
in Turkey"; and Frey, *op. cit.*
[57] Fainsod, *op. cit.*; Brzezinski, *op. cit.*; and Armstrong, *op. cit.*

they attempted. The major focuses of this transformation were overall social (only to a smaller degree national), revolutionary symbols, aiming at the total transformation of the symbols of identification of the society and establishing a new social order, based on the revolutionary ideological tenets.

These totalistic-ideological orientations of the communists could also be seen in the nature and extent of institutional transformation attempted by them.[58] This transformation was much more radical and extensive than in the preceding cases, and was based on a much higher element of coercion. A much stronger orientation to intensive and controlled change and control-oriented policies in the social, economic, and educational fields developed here.

These policies aimed at a series of significant structural transformations of the society. The two major focuses of such transformations were the attempts to open up the local—especially the rural—units of the population to participate in the new wider frameworks, and the channelization and control of the process of intensive urbanization and industrialization through education and growing mobility toward these industrial sectors.[59]

The predominance of the political controls, the totalistic-ideological orientation to change, as well as the inheritance of the former period of relative economic and social retardation, had several important structural effects on the process of modernization of communist Russia, and probably also of China.

First, the strong emphasis on industrialization inevitably gave rise to a growing differentiation and specialization in almost all spheres of the society. At the same time, however, it also gave rise to the development of large-scale bureaucratic organizations supervised by the political elite combining control over different areas and specialized activities.[60]

They attempted to implement such regulations and to minimize any open representative or public bodies and public opinion, with strong regulation of markets and minimization of the developments of any autonomous professional orientation and organization.

At the same time within the confines of political organization a relative occupational and status flexibility developed. Various elite, bureaucratic, and professional groups developed tendencies to ascriptive monopolization of upper positions to many social, economic, and educational prerogatives, but these tendencies were countered by the at-

[58] Black, ed., op. cit.

[59] G. F. Bereday, W. W. Brickman, and G. H. Read, eds., The Changing Soviet School: The Comparative Education Society Field Study in the USSR (Boston: Houghton Mifflin Company, 1960); N. De Witt, "Upheaval in Education," Problems of Communism, 7 (January 1959); and G. S. Counts, Khrushchev and the Central Committee Speak on Education (Pittsburgh: University of Pittsburgh Press, 1960).

[60] Fainsod, op. cit.; and Brzezinski, op. cit.

tempt of the top political leaders to break up these ascriptive bases and to maintain through predominance of the party some extent of continuous differentiation of status and power criteria.[61]

ABSORPTION OF CHANGES AND ORIENTATIONS OF PROTEST

The specific orientations of the ruling elites to change have of course greatly influenced the patterns of absorption of political change within the totalitarian regimes.[62] Here political, social, and economic change have been consciously and deliberately fostered and directed by the political elite, which at the same time attempts to minimize the autonomous political expression of various social groups and their *political* reaction to the changes initiated by the elite. The expression of political demands of these various groups has been carefully molded by the rulers within organizations over which they attempt to maintain almost complete control, and any attempts to break through this control have been looked upon by them as a very grave political aberration. The various social changes have been formulated as political goals of the regime, and their political contents and expressions set and controlled by the political elite.

Thus these regimes are characterized both by direction, manipulation, and control of change by the ruling elite, and by the minimization of the actual *political* expressions of the reactions of various groups to such changes.

The major media of political modernization, innovation, and decision making have accordingly been the party, the party leadership, and to some extent the bureaucracy, while the legislature has performed purely ritual functions, and the executive (as distinct from the party leadership), although important in several aspects, plays mainly only a secondary, routine role. Although the relations between the party and the bureaucracy are often delicate and precarious in these regimes, it is through the juxtaposition of these two that the major impetuses to change, as well as the control and manipulation of its expressions, are organized and institutionalized. The party leadership and the party usually tend to serve as the major centers of innovation and of active manipulation and mobilization of political support, while the bureaucracy tends more to deal with the routine administration of the new conditions generated by the changes initiated by the political leadership and the party.

The continuity of such fostered change and the regime's ability to control it are closely connected with the interweaving of interest groups and of social movements (very often nonexistent or suppressed) in the

---

[61] *Ibid.*
[62] *Ibid.;* and Armstrong, *op. cit.*

monolithic party framework. The almost total integration of interest groups and of the nuclei of social movements or public opinion in the party or their control by the bureaucracy is of crucial importance for the ability of the elite to manipulate and control the political expression of change. Any attempt on behalf of such groups to more autonomous public debate or presentation of their demands has usually been envisaged as a very serious potential threat to the existing regime, as potential breeding ground for eruptions, and hence has given rise to many repressive measures.

The continuity of these regimes is greatly dependent on the maintenance of a balance between repressive measures aimed at the minimization of autonomous political expression, and the flexibility and ability of the ruling elite to integrate changing demands and orientations into the framework of the party and the bureaucracy, and at the same time making these frameworks somewhat more flexible.

The eruptions in these regimes have been much less organized than those that developed in the constitutional regimes. Here they have mostly taken the form of activities or of underground nuclei, remnants, or new crystallization of social movements and some forces of free public opinion. On the whole these regimes did not encourage or facilitate the development of the more organized and articulated forms of eruption and political activity. Only lately there seem to have developed some first glimmerings of semilegitimation, or at least lack of full repression of some more overt protest articulation.

The major weakness of these regimes has been in the agricultural sector, where the apathy to modernization has only been reinforced by the coercive measures of collectivization. Second, various problems and difficulties have inevitably developed in other institutional spheres among the more modernized sectors also, especially with growing differentiation, urbanization, and industrialization.[63] Third, such regimes are usually threatened by the potentially secessional or usurpational tendencies of their apparatus, be they the army, the secret police, some parts of the bureaucracy, or even regional sectors of the party. As up to now we have no examples of internal systemic changes of totalitarian regimes except under the impact of defeat in war, it is impossible to designate either the exact range of the absorptive capacity or the types of regime that may succeed them. But here also, with growing development, industrialization, and bureaucratization, interesting structural transformations as well as new social problems tend to develop. These became very prominent in the Khrushchev and post-Khrushchev era.[64]

[63] S. N. Eisenstadt, "Modernization and Conditions of Sustained Growth," *World Politics*, 16, 4 (July 1964); and W. Leonard, *The Kremlin since Stalin*, trans. E. Wiskemann and M. Jackson (London: Oxford University Press, 1962).

[64] Leonard, *ibid.*; Brzezinski, *op. cit.*; and Armstrong, *op. cit.*

The growing routinization of the regime, the continuous industrialization and socio-economic development, the growth of new professional, bureaucratic, managerial, and cultural-literary groups, have created a growing pressure on the extension of the scope of benefits and security and growing demands for some autonomy and structural flexibility. All these changes have evidently given rise to some significant changes, with important social-structural implications, in the central political organs. The most important one has been the extension of some legitimation to more collegial arrangements, in which the interest of various groups can presumably be taken more into account.

These same changes have also given rise to the development of some types of social problem not dissimilar from those of other societies in later stages of industrialization. Among these most important are general social apathy and youth apathy in particular, as well as the development of some literary subcultures, and some more organized types of articulation of protest, such as strikes. These new types of orientations of protest together with the older, especially evident in the agricultural sector, constitute the most important focuses of social protest and change in these regimes.

The extent to which these regimes will be able to cope with these problems will greatly affect their future structural characteristics and continuity.

The Transformation of Colonial Societies

INITIAL MODERNIZING ORIENTATIONS OF COLONIAL POWERS

We shall now proceed to the analysis of processes of modernization in the so-called "new states"—i.e., those states which have gained their independence from colonial powers, especially since World War II. We have here the most extreme examples of processes of modernization induced by external forces. Here it was not only the initial response of the pre-existing centers and strata that were induced by external force, but also the very modern centers were initially established by such external force—by the colonial powers.

These powers developed specific orientation to change. They were, of course, interested in the promotion of change in the colonial societies, but at the same time saw it as part of their task to effect these changes only within very specific limits.[65]

They attempted to limit such changes to administrative and tech-

[65] Shils, *Political Development in the New States;* S. N. Eisenstadt, *Essays on the Sociological Aspects of Political and Economic Development* (The Hague: Mouton, 1961); and J. H. Kautsky, ed., *Political Change in Underdeveloped Countries: Nationalism and Communism* (New York: John Wiley & Sons, Inc., 1962).

nical as against deeper social and cultural spheres, and to the center as against the broader periphery. Most changes introduced either directly or indirectly by the colonial powers have been focused on the central institutions of the society. In the political field, the introduction of unitary systems of administration, the unification or regularization of taxation, the establishment of modern court procedures, and at later stages the introduction of limited types of representation, have greatly changed the overall political institutions and orientations. The changes have introduced certain universal criteria and orientations toward general rules and modern procedures. Even where various forms of indirect rule were practised (as in many British Southeast Asian and particularly African territories), some change inevitably took place in political organization, though this change was much slower than in cases of direct rule. Similarly, many changes have been effected in the economy, notably the change to a market economy, and in the educational field, by endeavoring to provide new types of modern education for selected local elites.

But at the same time the colonial rulers have not attempted to foster parallel changes within the broader strata of the society, especially at the local level, i.e., the level of the village, community, or tribal unit.[66] Here the colonial rulers attempted to contain most changes within the limits of traditional groups and to limit, as far as possible, the extent of any change. They tried to contain these changes on the local level within traditional systems. The broader strata were expected to perform various new roles, especially economic and administrative, while at the same time they were denied some of the basic rewards inherent in these settings. Above all, they were denied full participation in a common political system and full integration in a common system of solidarity. In other words, they were expected to act on the basis of a motivational system derived from a different social structure which the colonial powers and indigenous rulers tried to maintain. But on the local level this inevitably gave rise to varied processes of disorganization, de-tribalization and the like.[67]

Thus there tended to develop a basic contradiction: On the one hand, attempts were made to establish broad, modern administrative, political, and economic settings, while on the other hand, these changes were to be limited and based on relatively unchanged local and tribal groups and on traditional attitudes and loyalties. This contradictory attitude could be found in most spheres of social life. In the economic field, major efforts were made to facilitate the functioning of a market-oriented

[66] Eisenstadt, *ibid.*

[67] Eisenstadt, *Essays on the Sociological Aspects* . . . ; and G. T. McKahin, *Nationalism and Revolution in Indonesia* (Ithaca, N.Y.: Cornell University Press, 1953).

economy, of a very specific kind. This economy had to operate without full development of new economic motivations, which would have disturbed the existing social order. These relatively rapidly developing modern economies were distorted by their ties to the economic system of the metropolis, as they stimulated mainly the production of those products which the imperial economies could use. In the field of education, where innovations were on the whole more restricted, a tendency developed to impart rudiments of technical education without changing the system of values and aspirations.

These internal contradictions were most pronounced in the political field. Since the colonial powers or the indigenous rulers were interested in maintaining the political loyalty of the population, they aimed at maintaining a relatively passive type of obedience and identification, and were whenever possible ready to utilize existing traditional loyalties or to transfer them to the new setting without much change in their basic social and cultural orientations.[68]

UNBALANCED CHANGE IN COLONIAL SOCIETIES

Out of these orientations to change and basic policies of the colonial powers developed some of the major characteristics of the processes of change in these societies, the most important of which has been that the change was, from several points of view, continuously uneven and unbalanced. These processes of uneven change did not, during the colonial regime, stop at any given stage and freeze a colonial society's development. Many attempts were indeed made to freeze them, evidenced by the attempts at indirect rule, on the one hand, and by widespread efforts of colonial rulers to limit changes to purely technical matters, on the other. But such devices could not succeed for long. The economic needs of the colonial powers and/or of the indigenous ruling groups, their growing dependency on international markets, and on the international political system and the changes within it, precluded any freezing of development. The greater the tempo of these changes, the greater the unevenness and lack of balance, and the greater the problems of acute malintegration these political systems had to face.

Within the framework of these processes of unbalanced change—and largely in response to them—various new indigenous forces of modernization also developed. These were of several types. First there were those groups that were able to participate in the new educational institutions and to attain new positions in the colonial administration or in various

[68] H. Feith, *The Decline of Constitutional Democracy in Indonesia* (Ithaca, N.Y.: Cornell University Press, 1962).

professions.[69] Second were varied types of modern economic entrepreneurs, of different types and ranges of activities, stemming from various traditional business communities or coming up through modern and colonial enterprises.[70]

Third, and from the point of view of our analysis most important, has been the new political elite—the leaders of the various political, mostly national, movements.[71] They usually came from sectors of the more Westernized professional and intellectual groups, from among students, lawyers, journalists, most of whom had been directly exposed to Western values and had been active in some modern institutions, but either had not been fully absorbed by them or, though indoctrinated with Western ideologies and values, could not accept their nonrealization within the colonial setting.[72]

Most of the early leaders of nationalistic movements came from relatively well-to-do families. They had adapted themselves to some aspects of Western life, without entirely losing a foothold in their own traditions, and they rarely suffered from personal oppression. However, at later stages, the composition of these groups tended to change. These new men were mostly of urban origin; at least they grew up in the new urban settings that had come into being under the colonial regime.

In effect they were a typical—or perhaps an extreme—case of an intelligentsia. They were on the whole recruited from among these who underwent Western education but who were also, in greatly differing degrees in various countries, dissociated from their background, and constituted the only available westernized elite.

THE REPERCUSSION OF UNBALANCED CHANGE
IN THE POLITICAL SPHERE

The attitudes and social characteristics of these nationalistic movements were closely related to the social origins and processes of selection of their leaders, and to the relation of the leaders to the masses of the population.[73] Most of the national and social movements that developed

---

[69] W. A. Lewis, "Education and Economic Development," *Social and Economic Studies,* 10 (1961), 113-27; and L. G. Cowan, *The West African Intellectual Community,* published for the Congress for Cultural Freedom (Ibadan, Nigeria: Ibadan University Press, 1962).

[70] See for illustrative materials A. I. Richards, ed., *Economic Development and Tribal Change* (Cambridge: W. Heffer & Sons, Ltd., 1954); and D. Forde, ed., *Social Implications of Industrialization and Urbanization in Africa South of Sahara* (Paris: UNESCO, 1956).

[71] T. Hodgkin, *Nationalism in Colonial Africa* (New York: New York University Press, 1957); C. Kerr, *Industrialism and Industrial Man* (Cambridge, Mass.: Harvard University Press, 1960); E. Hagen, *On the Theory of Social Change* (Homewood, Ill.: Richard D. Irwin, Inc., 1962), esp. Chap. 10; Shils, *Political Development in the New States;* and Eisenstadt, *Essays on the Sociological Aspects. . . .*

[72] Shils, *ibid.*

[73] Hodgkin, *op. cit.;* and *ibid.*

in these situations were especially sensitive to the manifestations of lack of balance and evenness of change typical of the colonial activities. At the same time, they usually could not easily overcome the problems that this imbalance had created. This sensitivity can be discerned in two basic characteristics of these movements: first, in their strong emphasis on new secular, modern symbols of solidarity and on their strong orientation towards solidary-political activity (aiming ultimately at political independence); and second, in their attempts, especially in the later stages of development, to break through the "freezing" at the local level and reach the broad masses of the population. But at the same time, the common bond they tried to create with the masses was almost entirely couched in modern solidary-political terms, and did not emphasize the solution of immediate economic and administrative problems.[74]

True, most nationalist movements did develop an economic ideology, stressing either, romantically, the maintenance of the old village community or the necessity of state planning. All decried the injustice of the economic policies and discrimination by the colonial powers. But the nationalist leaders did not usually deal with concrete current economic problems or with problems of daily administration. It is significant that those social groups among colonial people who participated relatively successfully in economic or administrative areas and who developed new types of social organization (as, for example, native business communities or membership in the colonial services), usually did not participate actively in the nationalistic movements and often were looked upon as traitors, or at least as compromisers, by the members and leaders of these movements.[75]

Similarly, the modernizing orientations of these movements and their leaders were focused mostly on the political and much less on the cultural sphere, in the sense of redefinition and reformation of the basic internal value-orientations of these groups.[76]

Consequently the relations between the rising nationalistic elites and the wider strata of their societies were usually concentrated in the political sphere and to a much smaller degree in the economic and cultural spheres.[77] In most of the nonpolitical spheres—in the economic and cul-

---

[74] E. Shils, "The Concentration and Dispersion of Charisma: Their Bearing on Economic Policy in Underdeveloped Countries," *World Politics*, 10 (1958), 232-55; D. Apter, "The Role of Traditionalism in the Political Modernization of Ghana and Uganda," *World Politics*, 13, 1 (October 1960), 45-68; Eisenstadt, *Essays on the Sociological Aspects* . . . ; and Hodgkin, *op. cit.*

[75] *Ibid.*

[76] Shils, *Political Development in the New States;* and C. Geertz, ed., *Old Societies and New States* (New York: Free Press of Glencoe, Inc., 1963).

[77] H. Benda, "Non-Western Intelligentsias as Political Elites," in Kautsky, ed., *op. cit.*, pp. 235-51.

tural spheres—relatively few active modernizing groups tended to develop.

Even more problematic was the extent to which the major social groups or strata in these societies were able to develop from within themselves active orientations and resources for modernization and for becoming integrated into new wider frameworks. While all of them underwent processes of social disorganization in various spheres of social life, especially in the economic and social ones, the extent to which they were able to develop new autonomous orientations to modern frameworks and goals and to become integrated into wider, more flexible types of political frameworks was not very great; although naturally it varied between different societies or parts thereof.[78]

Thus most nationalistic movements, though obviously opposed to the colonial regime, inherited some important social characteristics from the preceding institutional setting. On the one hand, the leaders attempted to formulate new symbols of solidarity which would transcend the limitations of the colonial situation, and were couched in modern nationalistic and universalistic terms. But at the same time, they did not make great special efforts to transform other spheres of institutional life and to solve the problems created there by the processes of uneven change.[79]

The preceding characteristics of the nationalist movements in colonial countries were closely related to the weakness of various economic and professional organizations; e.g., trade unions, cooperatives, chambers of commerce; and the lack of their mutual integration, as well as their uneasy relationship with the political movements. These weaknesses usually were of two kinds. Either the economic organizations, whatever their strength, held themselves apart from one another and from the political movements, did not participate in them, and thus did not exert their influence on them; or they became entirely subordinate to the political leaders, who did not take account of the specific problems and needs of economic organizations.[80]

On the other hand, the various interest groups, such as local merchants, exerted influence on the administration or on political organizations in lower levels of government, mostly through lobbying, personal pressure, and sometimes attempts at bribery. Whatever the exact nature and diversity of these activities, they were not closely related to the major political movements and did not to any great extent envisage the mobilization of public opinion. Whenever one of these issues became im-

[78] Geertz, ed., *op. cit.*

[79] Kautsky, ed., *op. cit.;* Shils, *Political Development in the New States;* and R. Emerson, "The Erosion of Democracy in the New States," in H. Eckstein and D. Apter, eds., *Comparative Politics: A Reader* (New York: Free Press of Glencoe, Inc., 1963), pp. 635-55.

[80] Richards, ed., *op cit.;* and D. Forde, *op. cit.*

portant for political groups and public opinion, it became transformed into an overall problem of political independence and subsumed under the general solidarity symbols.

The combination of all these factors perhaps explains the importance of the urban "mob" in the politics of many colonial countries—and the parallel weakness of organized public opinion.[81]

TRANSFORMATION OF MODERNIZING ATTITUDES

The nature of the relations between the modernizing elites and the wider social groups has become transformed in these countries with the attainment of independence; but this very transformation was greatly influenced by the basic characteristics of their initial modernization, analyzed above.

The leaders of the nationalistic groups have become ruling elites, officially bent on overall modernization of their countries and faced with the double problem of establishing new political frameworks, institutions, and consensus and of keeping themselves in power. The attainment of political independence and the establishment of a new state always entailed the establishment of new spheres of power [82] and gave rise to the promotion of new collective symbols of identification, mostly borne by the new political elites, which also claimed special acceptance and legitimation because of their participation in the struggle for independence and because of the successful attainment of this aim.[83]

These claims have usually been closely related to the orientations to change and modernization that were developed by most of the leaders of the new nations.

The emphasis on change, progress, and economic development is one of the main tenets of their political and ideological orientations. But at the same time, their institutional capacity to absorb changes may be disproportionately small compared to their aspirations for change, although it necessarily varies greatly among the different new states according to varied conditions, some of which will be discussed later.[84] This relatively small extent of institutional ability to absorb change— even sometimes to maintain their own positions—is manifest in the weakness of the administration, in the lack of the stability and continuity of

[81] L. W. Pye, "Communication Patterns and the Problems of Representative Government in Non-Western Societies," *Public Opinion Quarterly,* **20** (Spring 1956), 249-57.

[82] Kautsky, ed., *op. cit.*

[83] Shils, *Political Development in the New States;* and Eisenstadt, *Essays on the Sociological Aspects. . . .*

[84] Kautsky, ed., *op. cit.;* Shils, *ibid.;* and M. Nash, "Some Social and Cultural Aspects of Economic Development," *Economic Development and Cultural Change,* **7,** 2 (January 1959), 137-51.

basic symbols and of administrative and political frameworks, and also in the relative weakness and underdevelopment of various autonomous interest groups.[85]

In order to be able to understand these potential weaknesses we should analyze the basic characteristics of the centers and periphery that tended to develop in these societies.

BASIC STRUCTURAL CHARACTERISTICS OF CENTERS AND PERIPHERY

Within the political centers, there developed first strong tendencies toward an emphasis on the executive, on the one hand, and toward single or dominant parties, which encompass most types of political organizations, on the other—both of which tend to serve as agencies of social change. The strong emphasis on the executive is seen in most of the constitutions of the new African states that invest the head of state of government with very far-reaching constitutional powers, within which there is a growing tendency to single or dominant-party regimes. Similarly, in Indonesia we witness the development—after the failure of the constitutional regime—of a presidential regime, while in Pakistan and Burma a military regime developed after initial failure.[86]

Second, and closely related with the former tendency, is the great importance of the governmental and political sector in the modern sectors of economy. While the concrete contours of this sector greatly differ between various new states, some common features can be discerned. Government corporations, centrally controlled large-scale cooperatives, and various enterprises run directly by the government or the party can be found in varied degrees, as very important, if not the most important, parts of the indigenous (as distinct from the foreign) modern economic sectors.[87]

Third is the development, within the modern sectors of these so-

[85] *Ibid.*
[86] On Indonesia, see Feith, *op. cit.;* and W. A. Hannah, *Bung Karno's Indonesia* (New York: American Universities Field Staff, 1961). On Pakistan, see K. B. Sayeed, "The Collapse of Parliamentary Democracy in Pakistan," *Middle East Journal,* 13, 4 (1959), 389-406; R. Wheeler, "Pakistan: New Constitution, Old Issues," *Middle East Journal,* 13, 4 (1959); and K. Callard, *Pakistan: A Political Study* (New York: The Macmillan Company, 1957). On Burma, see E. R. Leach, "L'avenir Politique de la Birmanie," *Bull Sedeis* (Paris: Futuribles, November 1962); L. W. Pye, *Politics, Personality and Nation Building* (New Haven: Yale University Press, 1962); and J. H. Badgley, "Burma: The Nexus of Socialism and Two Political Traditions," *Asian Survey,* 3, 2 (February 1963), 89-96.
[87] B. Glassburner, "Economic Policy-Making in Indonesia: 1950-1957," *Economic Development and Cultural Change,* 10, 2 (January 1962), 113-133; and J. C. Mackie, "Indonesia's Government Estates and Their Masters," *Pacific Affairs,* 34, 4 (Winter 1961-62), 337-60.

cieties, of relatively large-scale, highly bureaucratic organization and of the attempts to subsume many smaller groups such as trade unions or various types of voluntary associations, within the framework of unified political party units.[88]

Some of the structural characteristics of the broader groups stand out against these characteristics of the center. First is the relatively low level of social mobilization or differentiation, as measured either by socio-demographic indices or by the extent and scope of social differentiation. The predominance of primary occupations in general, of traditional farming in particular, the low level of industrialization, all attest to this fact.[89] But this low level of differentiation was connected with intensive processes of change, with rapid de-tribalization and urbanization. Hence, in many cases when these broader groups became disorganized and socially mobilized, and drawn into the orbit of the new central modern institutions, they tended to evince the characteristics of closeness and excessive political orientations and demands similar to those we have encountered above in the Latin American countries. Closely related to those characteristics is the tendency to profusion of relatively small-scale, often ephemeral, types of social groupings, which are to no small degree connected with the processes of change and with the breakdown of various traditional units.[90]

All these processes influence the class structure of these societies, even beyond the great differences among them, and evince some special characteristics.

This "class" structure is probably the steepest one among all the societies surveyed here, this steepness being accentuated by the differences between the traditional and the modern sectors, the heavy predominance of the agrarian element in the traditional sector, by the continuous disorganization of the traditional center, and by the heavy preponderance of government oriented and bureaucratic class formation in the modern center.

Another important aspect of the process of modernization of the broader social groups in most new states is the relative sequence of modernization in different institutional spheres—the relatively quick development of the political aspirations of the wider social groups and their overall political modernization before a concomitant extent of economic,

---

[88] A. Southall, ed., *Social Change in Modern Africa* (London: Oxford University Press, 1961); and G. Carter, ed., *African One-party States* (Ithaca, N. Y.: Cornell University Press, 1962).

[89] K. Deutsch, "Social Mobilization and Political Development," *American Political Science Review*, **55** (September 1961), 494-95; and *Report on the World Social Situation* (New York: United Nations, 1963).

[90] Forde, *op. cit.;* and Southall, *op. cit.*

professional, and often even educational development. The high level of modernization of political demands, in its turn, usually gave rise to a quicker development of educational facilities and aspirations—especially of the more generalized and humanistic ones—which often outstripped the economic facilities.[91]

Because of all these characteristics most of the new states evince the most extreme synchronization and coalescence of the characteristics and problems of the societies analyzed in this part of the book—of low levels of local mobilization and of internal transformation of wider groups, of high level of their politization, and of the concomitant formation of new political centers in these difficult conditions.

STRATIFICATION AND IDEOLOGY

The synchronization of these different characteristics—of the special temporal sequence of modernization in different spheres, of the relatively low initial level of differentiation coupled together with the concomitant building up of new centers—points out the great importance of the processes and structures that bring together the traditional and more modern sectors.

Of special importance are some characteristics of the new emerging system of social stratification, especially as it bears on processes of transition from the traditional to the modern sectors. As has already been pointed out, the range or scope of the modern sector is relatively small, although it is continually expanding. But this very expansion displays certain specific characteristics.

First, it is because of the predominance of the government, on the whole more heavily concentrated in the administrative and political than in the business, professional, or purely economic areas in the economy.[92] Second, two channels of mobility to upper positions, often overlapping, usually seem to be of special importance. One is educational and the other political.[93]

Although there is as yet little adequate evidence, there is some indication that the importance of the educational channel is constantly on the rise and that the more it becomes an important avenue of mobility, the greater becomes the pressure on educational facilities and the smaller the return on investment in education—especially insofar as the modern occu-

[91] Lewis, "Education and Economic Development"; J. Fischer, "Universities and the Political Process in South-East Asia," *Pacific Affairs*, 36, 1 (Spring 1963), 3-16; H. Mint, "The Universities of South-East Asia and Economic Development," *Pacific Affairs*, 35, 2 (Summer 1962), 116-28; and Eisenstadt, *Education and Political Development*.

[92] G. Carter, *op. cit.*; E. Shils, "Political Development in New States," *op. cit.*

[93] See footnote 91.

pational sector does not expand to the same degree as the educational system and the access to it.

There are also few adequate data on the differential access to educational facilities, but existing data seem to indicate that while there develops, as in most other modern countries, a tendency for sons of well-to-do (urban and educated) people to have greater chances of educational advancement, on the whole there is a relatively large extent of openness and accessibility of the educational positions to sons of other (especially farming) groups.[94]

Thus in many of these countries there tends to develop a combination of relatively restricted scope and nature of the upper positions in the modern sector, as against a relatively broader base from which the recruitment to these positions takes place.

The process of crystallization of new frameworks or mechanisms which could serve as bridges between the new centers and the broader periphery has also been evident in the search for new symbols of common cultural identity.

Several dimensions or poles of this search stand out. One is that of "tradition vs. modernity," and the search for those elements in the specific historical heritage of societies that may best contribute to the crystallization of new, more flexible, specifically Asian or African symbols of modernity.[95] Another is the search for a possible crystallization of a meaningful personal and collective identity transcending any given particularistic collectivity. Perhaps the search for African personality is the best illustration, if not necessarily solution, of this search.[96] The last dimension of this search can be seen in the attempts at the incorporation of the several different historical, religious, and ideological traditions—the specific historical heritage of these societies, the broad religious orientation brought by Buddhism, Christianity, and Islam—into the new national, international, and social ideologies. It is around these varied dimensions and confrontations that the attempts focused to forge out new symbols of collective identity.[97]

[94] R. J. Havighurst, "Education, Social Mobility and Social Change in Four Societies: A Comparative Study," *International Review of Education,* **4,** 2 (1958), 167-85; and Lewis, "Education and Economic Development."

[95] B. Hoselitz, "Tradition and Economic Growth," in R. Braibanti and J. Spengler, eds., *Tradition, Values and Socio-Economic Development* (Durham, N. C.; Duke University Press, 1961), pp. 83-113; and H. Feith, "Indonesia's Political Symbols and Their Wielders," *World Politics,* **16,** 1 (October 1963), 79-98.

[96] E. Maphalele, *The African Image* (New York: Frederick A. Praeger, Inc., 1962); and The First International Conference of Negro Writers, *Présence Africaine,* N.S., 8, 9, 10 (Paris, June-November 1956).

[97] P. E. Sigmund, Jr. *The Ideologies of the Developing Nations* (New York: Frederick A. Praeger, Inc., 1963); and F. R. Von der Mehden, "The Changing Pattern of Religion and Politics in Burma," in *Studies on Asia* (Lincoln, Nebr.: University of Nebraska Press, 1961), II, 63-73; M. Sarkisyanz, "On the Place of U Nu's Buddhist Socialism in Burma's History of Ideas," in *ibid.,* pp. 53-62; and Feith, "Indonesia's Political Symbols and Their Wielders," *op. cit.*

MAJOR PROBLEMS OF INTEGRATION

The crystallization of the various structural characteristics of modernization analyzed above points out some primal problems and potential weaknesses of the emerging centers in the new states. The most important of these weaknesses have been connected with the problems and ways of the opening up of the broader strata in the direction of growing modernization, especially in the economic field, and of the ways of linking them up to the modern centers, and the possibility to regulate them.

All the ruling elites of the new states initiated manifold policies of social mobilization in the economic, educational, and political fields, which in their broad formal outlines were not dissimilar from those of the more revolutionary elites of Turkey or Mexico.

But here, as in several other countries discussed above—e.g., many of the Latin American countries—there often developed, both from within the broader groups and from within the new elites themselves, different, often contradictory tendencies and possibilities.

Within the broader groups the major problem was the extent to which their opening up under the impact of the policies first of the colonial powers and later of their own elites was connected, with some degree of internal value transformation; or, conversely, with their closeness and with the concomitant growth of unregulated political demands and aspirations.

The policies undertaken by the elites also very often oscillated between constructive efforts at establishing new viable modern institutions and regulating the tempo and direction of modernization within relatively realistic and consistent frameworks; or, conversely, to the continual giving in to, and even fostering of new demands that could not be dealt with at all, which tended to undermine the existing frameworks.[98]

These tendencies have often been connected with strong orientation of the elites to self-aggrandizement and to the maintenance of their own positions of power and prestige, and the erosion of commitments to collective and developmental goals.

The crucial test of all these regimes at this stage is the extent to which the policies undertaken by the elites and the political orientation of the broader strata may facilitate or impede the development of relatively flexible channels and frameworks interlinking the center and the broader periphery, and create political and ideological or value systems within a flexible or a frozen and rigid status.

Both such status flexibility and the opposite tendencies to ascriptive freezing of structural arrangements can be found in all spheres of social

[98] Hannah, op. cit.; R. Butwell, "The Four Failures of U Nu's Second Premiership," Asian Survey, 11, 1 (March 1962), 3-12; and references in footnote 96.

organizations—in political parties, labor organizations, different areas and channels of mobility—and are not necessarily tied to any specific structural form or level of development.

From the point of view of the development of these possibilities, four broad areas seem to be of very great importance. The first is the extent of continuous economic development and differentiation, diversification, and some weakening of its dependence on the former metropolis, very simple and yet basic preconditions of further development—a necessary if not sufficient condition of structural flexibility within the emerging modern frameworks.[99]

Second are the processes of recrystallization within the traditional frameworks, and the concomitant processes of religious and ideological transformation that have been taking place. These processes of religious reorganization and recrystallization contain on the one hand important possibilities of development of orientation to wider, more flexible, and differentiated activities and goals, while on the other hand they may also contribute to the crystallization of some more flexible and cohesive symbols of collective identity.[100]

Third is the process of political transformation itself, with the strong drive to the center that implies such possibilities of transformation, although at the same time, with regard to the other spheres mentioned above, it may contain many possibilities of rigidity and breakdown.[101]

The fourth area, the development of which is crucial for sustained growth, is that of education. We have already seen that education provides one of the most important channels of transition from the traditional to the modern sectors in African societies. Therefore, it is but natural that its structure and organization can greatly affect the whole process of modernization.[102]

From this point of view two aspects of the developing educational systems seem to be of greatest importance. The first is the extent of heterogeneity and variety of the educational system, the lack of rigid adherence to a narrow academic or legalistic schooling system, the development of varied educational programs, and the consequent facilitation by the educational system of creation of a more flexible and dynamic status order. The other important aspect is the nature of the interrelation

[99] S. N. Eisenstadt, *Modernization, Growth and Diversity,* Carnegie faculty seminar (Bloomington, Ind.: Department of Government, Indiana University, 1963).

[100] C. Geertz, "Ideology as a Cultural System," in D. Apter, ed., *Contemporary Ideology: Problems of Role and Method* 1963, Yearbook in Political Science; C. Geertz, "Primordial Sentiments and Civil Policies in the New States," in C. Geertz, ed., *op. cit.*

[101] *Ibid., ibid.*

[102] Eisenstadt, *Education and Political Development;* J. Foster, "Ethnicity and the School in Ghana," *Comparative Education Review,* **6,** 2 (October 1962), 127ff; and Tiryakian, *op. cit.*

between educational expansion and the general direction and tempo of economic and social development and modernization.

Educational systems and planners are faced here with two basic, to some extent contradictory possibilities and dilemmas. One possibility is the development of a relatively conservative stagnative educational system, geared mostly to the needs and self-image of a relatively small, restricted elite and losing most of its dynamic innovative and change-oriented potentialities. The other is that of a rigid, undifferentiated expansion of the educational system outstripping the realistic possibilities of their societies.[103]

The various processes analyzed above tend to explain some of the major difficulties these states face in implementing the aspirations of their rulers to bring about far-reaching social and economic changes and transformations. The focus of these difficulties is the fact that the rulers of these countries, more than rulers of other types of regimes hitherto discussed, are faced with the simultaneous development of rather different and often contradicting problems, the solution of which may greatly influence the extent of institutionalization of stable modern political systems. They are faced first with the problem of creation and a general identification with the new polity, with the maintenance of general, sustained interest in different complex political issues and problems, and with mobilization of support for its own program. A new elite is faced second with acquisition of power or with maintaining itself in power, and third, with finding adequate ways and means of solving various outstanding social, economic, and political problems. Insofar as these aspects of developing political orientations reinforce one another, the prospects for the development of a realistic and critical attitude toward political issues, and for the possibility of getting political support in terms of realistic programs, are relatively great. But insofar as these different political orientations contradict one another—and such a possibility is to some extent inherent in some of the basic conditions of these states—various unrealistic and destructive attitudes toward political life, and different types of eruptions can easily develop.[104]

Here the tension or confrontation between the formation of new modern states and new symbols of national identity tends to develop in a very special, probably most extreme, form.

Here is but little opposition between the state, the political center, and the national movement. Rather the problem is the objective weakness of

[103] Fischer, *op. cit.;* and S. N. Eisenstadt, "Education and Political Development," in C. Piper and T. Cole, eds., *Postprimary Education and Political and Economic Development* (Durham, N.C.: Duke University Press, 1964).

[104] Shils, *Political Development in the New States;* Eisenstadt, *Essays on the Sociological Aspects of Economic and Political Development;* and D. Lerner, "Towards a Communication Theory of Modernization," in L. W. Pye, ed., *Communication and Political Development* (Princeton, N.J.: Princeton University Press, 1963), pp. 327-51.

both of them. The new political center is mostly a heritage of the colonial regime, and although it has been taken over by the new ruling elite it commands, on the whole, little civil allegiance and identification.

The symbols of new national identity have to be forged out of a great variety of tribal, provincial, or caste traditions that still command the allegiance of wider groups of the population, frequently cut across political boundaries, and are often borne by relatively weak modernized groups.

Although the new elite is usually interested in fostering the allegiance to both the political center and the symbols of nationhood, yet its ability to do so may be small, and moreover each may become a focus of separate, conflicting loyalties.

The high level of political demands, the possible cleavages among the elites in their pursuit of popular support, may easily create conditions under which they themselves are unable to assure the initial institutionalization of political frameworks capable of absorption of change.

This discrepancy between the strong emphasis on change and the relative weakness of the institutional frameworks that have to absorb them can be seen in the nature of the eruptions that develop in these regimes after the initial stages of independence. These eruptions are characterized by a combination of very primitive outbreaks and outbursts on the one hand, with much more organized and articulated eruptions in the form of organized social and political movements on the other. The exact nature, scope, and persistence of these eruptions, as well as the regime's ability to absorb them, varies greatly between these various new states, and of course may greatly influence their stability and continuity.[105]

The crucial stage for all these regimes comes when the various new political forces—i.e., forces not fully represented by the original nationalist elite, be they regional, trade unions, or new rural leaders, or the older traditional ones—emerge, often through the policies of development of the nationalist elites, and create, through their demands, potential splits within the elite and strains on the working of the central institutions.

It is out of these varied elements that new orientations of protest and of different structural possibilities, breakdowns, stagnation, or transformation tend to develop. They may create, through their demands, potential splits within the elite and strains on the working of the central institutions—and pose the problem of the conditions under which the new centers, with their specific structural characteristics, will be able to facilitate sustained growth and development.

[105] *Ibid., ibid.*

SOME MAJOR DIFFERENCES AMONG THE NEW STATES

Beyond these common characteristics and problems of the new states, there obviously also exist many great differences among them, with regard to their structural characteristics, the acuteness of their problems, and their ability to deal with them.

The various new states may be distinguished first according to composition and major social and political orientation of their respective elites. Shils has distinguished here between the traditional oligarchy, various types of modernizing oligarchies (civil or military), totalitarian regimes, and tutelary democracies.[106] Of these, naturally, traditional oligarchy and some of the modernizing ones seem least predisposed to change, while the others seem to be most oriented to the promotion of change.

But the ability of the ruling elites of these states to deal with these problems, and their response to the various challenges analyzed above, depends not only on their initial modernizing attitude but also on some aspects of their composition and structure, which may also cut across these various types.

Of special importance here is the extent to which the modernizing elites are relatively strong, cohesive, differentiated, and flexible, and can mobilize adequate support from different strata without giving rise by this very process to new cleavages within the society and undermining the cohesion of its major strata.

Similarly, the stronger and more cohesive internally are the major strata, and the more they are able to participate in the process of modernization in various institutional spheres, the greater is the extent of resources they are able to put at the disposal of various modern institutions and organizations. The greater also is their ability to regulate through autonomous mechanisms some of the problems attendant on the growing differentiation and modernization, to articulate realistic political demands, and to influence the formulation of major political goals and policies by the elites.

Many factors may influence the extent to which such various forces of strength develop in new states. Of special importance is the extent to which traditions of relatively strong centers, differentiation, and institutional flexibility that could be transposed into the modern settings that existed within the autochthonous and/or colonial societies. Such traditions, and the possibility of their transposition to modern settings, might have been fostered either by the autochthonous, precolonial social order and/or by the specific impact of the colonial setting on this social order.

[106] Shils, *Political Development in the New States,* esp. Part III.

We can only analyze this process briefly as it has developed in the new state that has until now shown the greatest success in maintaining a new, modern institutional center and political framework—India.[107]

From the point of view of our discussion, the first important feature of Indian civilization is the fact that it has been a complex and highly differentiated historical one that maintained its cultural entity throughout the march of history without being tied to any given political framework. This is true not only of the last centuries of Muslim rule and later English rule, but even before that. Although small and large states and imperial centers did develop in India, no single state developed with which the cultural tradition was identified.

This basic characteristic of Indian civilization had a very important influence on the structure and orientation of the initial processes of modernization, which began under the aegis of the British and continued under the national movement. This modern center was established first of all in terms of Western symbols, and was to some extent detached from the great Indian cultural tradition. True, with the Gandhian phase of the Indian national movement, its political aspirations became to some extent couched in traditional symbols, or at least were legitimized by some reinterpretation of such symbols; but this did not create any very specific or intensive demands (as was the case in Islam) on the institutional structure—except demands for independence and political justice, which were crouched mostly in Western terms.

This partial detachment of the modern political center from the traditional did not, at least initially, constitute a point of weakness. The dissociation could be at least partially legitimized in terms of the traditional ideological associations. Some of the symbols or values of the new center, such as justice, could be legitimized in terms of the older orientation of classical Indian political thought, and similarly could be found between this center and the internal reformist tendencies that developed among the upper layers of Hindu society.

Significantly, this new political-ideological center was, in the pre-Gandhian phase and even later, crystallized to a large extent by people coming from those groups or strata, especially the Brahman groups, that were the bearers of the great historical tradition in its nonpolitical aspects and emphases.[108]

The second important aspect of Indian society is the internal cohesion

[107] See in greater detail S. N. Eisenstadt, "Transformation of Social, Political and Cultural Orders in Modernization," *American Sociological Review*, 30, 5, (October 1965), 659-674.

[108] P. Spear, *India: A Modern History* (Ann Arbor, Mich.: University of Michigan Press, 1961); and H. N. Sinha, *The Development of Indian Polity* (Bombay: India Publishing House, 1963).

of broader social groups and strata, which evinced one of the highest degrees of autonomy in terms of internal identity and relation to the political order.

Not only were the cultural traditions independent of the political center, but the whole complex of castes, villages, and the various networks of cultural communication were to a high degree autonomous and self-regulating, with only limited recourse to the political center or centers. Similarly, the broader strata could absorb through their own mechanisms some of the problems of modernization, without either becoming immediately disorganized or creating excessive demands on the political center. These varied social groupings had their own strong orientation to broader cultural values, and legitimized their own identity in cultural rather than political terms.[109]

This had several important repercussions on the process of modernization. Perhaps the most important was the fact that the new modern political center could develop without strong and immediate impingement of intensive demands on it; a fact that stands out when the Indian situation is compared with that of many of the new states, where the impingement of broader groups on the center may be so strong that it does not allow the center to crystallize at all. The fact that this did not happen in India has greatly facilitated the development of the small groups, first under the influence of the British and then in national movement, through the Congress, the central institutional structure which evolved a vitality and stability of its own and operated to maintain some order and modern activity and to approach gradually its own expansion toward the broader groups.

These developments also contained two points of weakness. The first was that the center, while institutionally and organizationally strong and flexible, did not develop strong common symbols in which elements of both the new and the older cultural traditions could be combined, and which could create relatively strong commitments and identity. This becomes extremely important when the center extended the scope of its activities and of its dependence on the broader groups. Then the lack of close relations between the cultural tradition and political framework, which was a point of strength in the beginning, may become a point of weakness.

Here the two major problems stand out. One is the extent to which it is possible to forge out new binding symbols of identity, which can overcome the more parochial (mostly linguistic) symbols of the different

[109] V. P. Varma, *Studies in Hindu Political Thought and Its Metaphysical Background* (Benares, 1954); D. M. Brown, ed., *Indian Political Thought from Ranade to Bhave* (Berkeley, Calif.: University of California Press, 1962); and S. A. Wolfert, *Tilak and Gohale in Revolution and Reform in the Making of Modern India* (Berkeley, Calif.: University of California Press, 1962).

regions and states and develop some feeling of political community. This is especially acute as these parochial symbols tend also to become more crystallized and articulated with the growing modernization and politicization of the periphery. The explosive potentiality of the linguistic question in India is highly indicative of this problem.[110]

Second is the problem of to what extent there will develop, within the broad cultural tradition and within its reformative tendencies, not only permissiveness, which would allow the setting up of new institutional frameworks under external influence and the continuous recrystallization and adaptation of the traditional groups, but also new innovative forces, which could support institution building and the development of new, common integrative frameworks and organizations. Of special importance here is the problem of the extent to which the recrystallization of caste and other traditional groupings will facilitate the development of new, more flexible frameworks and cross-cuttings of different hierarchies of status within which new values and orientation activities may develop; or, conversely, to what extent it will reinforce the crystallization of new traditional divisive symbols and groupings.[111]

In many other New States a much greater variety of backgrounds and of initial modern situations developed, on which we shall comment here only briefly.

In some cases, as in Burma,[112] Indonesia,[113] or Pakistan,[114] we find situations in which there did indeed exist a relatively strong traditional center and a relatively complex social structure—with little internal flexibility, however, out of which there did not develop many effective links between the new centers and the broader groups and strata.

It is here that there developed, within the new states, the most extreme manifestations of situations of breakdown, which will be described in detail later. Here the various social and political developments characteristic of the new states, described above, have precipitated a downfall of the initial constitutional regime, giving rise to new political frameworks, centered mainly around the army of bureaucracy with a much smaller scope for political and social flexibility.

---

[110] M. Singer, ed., *Traditional India: Structure and Change* (Philadelphia: American Folklore Society, 1959); M. N. Srinivas, *Caste in Modern India* (Bombay: Asia Publishing House, 1962), esp. Chaps. 1, 2, 4; A. Beteille, *Closed and Open Social Stratification* (New Delhi, 1965); R. Kothari and A. Maru, *Caste and Secularism in India: A Case Study of a Caste Federation* (New Delhi, 1965); and L. I. Rudolph and S. H. Rudolph, "The Political Role of India's Caste Associations," *Pacific Affairs*, 33, 1 (March 1960), 5-22.

[111] S. Harrison, *India: The Most Dangerous Decades* (Princeton, N.J.: Princeton University Press, 1960); and P. Friedrich, "Language and Politics in India," *Daedalus* (Summer 1962).

[112] See footnote 86.

[113] See footnotes 86 and 87.

[114] See footnote 86.

As against these societies we find those—such as many of the African ones [115]—where the initial level of differentiation has been very small, in which there barely existed any strong, differentiated centers; which in many ways start almost from scratch, and within which therefore the general problem of modernization of new states described above may be felt in perhaps the most acute way.

[115] J. S. Coleman and C. G. Rosberg, eds., *Political Parties and National Integration in Tropical Africa* (Berkeley, Calif.: University of California Press, 1964); and Carter, ed., *op. cit.*

The preceding analysis of various case studies of modern and modernizing societies has shown us how the patterns of interaction among several of the major aspects of modernization —the different levels of differentiation of the social structure, the different historical starting points of modernization, the basic orientations of the major modernizing elites, and the differential tempo of modernization in the major institutional spheres of a society—explain to at least some extent the specific structural patterns of different modernizing regimes, their basic orientations to change as well as the differential capacity of these regimes for absorption of change. Yet there is, in principle, nothing preordained in the development and institutionalization of any such specific pattern or regime.

As we have seen, some basic problems are posed by the broad, general processes of modernization, and the specific constellation of these problems may differ greatly at different stages or in different situations of modernization. But the solution that tends to develop in any given case is not preordained. At any stage or in any situation of modernization, response to the problems created by the processes of social mobilization and differentiation may take several different forms.

The crystallization of such different institutional orders or solutions is shaped by the interaction between the broader structural features of the major institutional spheres, on

CHAPTER SIX

A Comparative Analysis of Situations
of Breakdown and of Sustained Growth

129

the one hand, and on the other, the development of elites or entrepreneurs in some of the institutional spheres of the society, in some of its enclaves, or even in other societies with which it is in some way connected—but in any given situation there always exist several different elites that compete among themselves for the position of predominance in the society, and different groups or strata that compete for influence over the elites; and there is always some degree of freedom with regard to the ultimate crystallization of any institutional patterns.

Once any such pattern becomes institutionalized, however, it develops its own specific cultural characteristics. Among these characteristics are also different patterns of eruptions and different degrees of the ability of the emerging modern institutional structure to deal with these eruptions, to absorb continual change, to assure sustained growth.

The great variety of eruptions that tend to develop in every modern and modernizing society has been brought out throughout the analysis of the various case studies. We have encountered such eruptions in the pockets of resistance to modernization in France, in the more intensive breakdowns of modern frameworks in Germany and Japan, and in various manifestations of structural duality in Latin America in the Thirties, as well as in the varied breakdowns in the new states.

What are the major structural forms and outcomes of such eruptions? Insofar as these eruptions did become crystallized in some way they evinced certain common characteristics despite the great variety of their concrete manifestations. The most important and general of these characteristics is the development, around some of the major themes of protest, of inclinations toward a more homogeneous, totalistic social and cultural order, with strong attempts at de-differentiation and/or withdrawal from participation in the more differentiated, modern social, economic, and political frameworks.

But such continuous crystallization of the social or cultural expressions of protest need not mean that they always give rise to structural, organizational breakdowns of the overall modern or modernized institutional structure. It is only when some such extreme manifestations of social, political, or cultural protest become closely combined with various manifestations of structural breakdown or disorganization that they may both contribute to such breakdown and become its symbolic expression. Similarly, the eruption or intensification of social problems, ubiquitous as they are in the processes of modernization, do not in themselves necessarily entail the breakdowns of the processes of modernization. It is only when they become entwined with other, more structural aspects of breakdowns that they tend both to become symbols of such overall breakdown and to contribute to them. The extent of their effects on the social settings in which they occur, of course, differs greatly from case to case.

POSSIBLE OUTCOMES OF ERUPTIONS

Most of these situations are characterized by a persistence of some basic characteristics of structural duality, combined with relative low effectiveness of the central institutions. But their concrete contours may vary greatly.

One major type of structural outcome of continuous eruption is the development and/or continuation of various institutional structures or organizations at relatively low levels of internal differentiation, incapable of maintaining a relatively stable internal and external relationship with or in more differentiated settings.

Several examples of such developments can be given. One is a continuous disorganization and depletion of various groups or strata, especially of the more traditional or lower ones, and of more active elements, and a concomitant gradual lowering of their overall level of functioning and efficiency.[1] This can be found in many rural areas under pressure of immigration and colonial rule, or in urban settings into which various rural groups may be transposed.

The second manifestation of such structural disorganization or breakdown, which may to some extent overlap with the first, is the maintenance by different rural, urban, professional, or other types of groups of a continuously low level of activity and of interrelation, limited mostly to adaptive relations with other groups and with wider setting.[2]

Such closeness and stagnation may very easily give rise to the development of delinquent communities, i.e., communities not oriented to the attainment of their manifest goals (be they economic growth, community development, or the like) but to the maintenance of the vested status and interest positions of their members within the existing settings.[3]

The third aspect or type of such disorganization is the development of a situation of internal war and conflict within a society. Such a situation may manifest itself in relatively nonarticulate eruptions, outbreaks in situations of unregulated conflicts, or development of various types of social movements—social, cultural, national—incapable of becoming absorbed within more stable frameworks.[4]

[1] E. C. Banfield, *The Moral Basis of a Backward Society* (New York: Free Press of Glencoe, Inc., 1958); M. Fried, "Grieving for a Lost Home," in L. J. Duhl, ed., *People and Policy in the Metropolis* (New York: Basic Books, Inc., Publishers, 1963), pp. 151-72; and H. J. Gans, *The Urban Villagers* (New York: Free Press of Glencoe, Inc., 1962).

[2] G. Germani, *Política y Sociedad en una época de transición* (Buenos Aires: Ed. Paidos, 1962).

[3] J. R. Pitts, "Continuity and Change in Bourgeois France," in S. H. Hoffman, ed., *In Search of France* (Cambridge, Mass.: Harvard University Press, 1963), pp. 254-59.

[4] M. Kaplan, ed., *The Revolution in World Politics* (New York: John Wiley & Sons, Inc., 1962), esp. Part II, "Protest Movements in Developed Areas," and Part III,

Fourth, there is the "freezing" of the more extreme expressions of protest as distinct social and organizational entities, in the form of sectarian movements, parties, and the like.

These varied orientations and outcomes of disorganization may become partially institutionalized or stabilized in parts and sectors of a society, e.g., within certain regional or occupational groups or strata, as continuous pockets of disorganization, or of delinquent communities.

They may also, however, become manifest in the overall institutional frameworks of societies, especially in their political structure, and give rise to overall restructuring of such frameworks. Such restructuring of overall institutional frameworks may develop in several different directions.

One major type of such recrystallization is the establishment of a relatively stagnating, regressive regime, i.e., of an institutional structure on a lower level of differential, which is not capable to cope with the manifold problems and processes of change that have developed in its preceding or initial situation. In several new nations, such as Burma or Indonesia,[5] as we have seen, where modern frameworks were initially established in different institutional fields, especially in the political one, not only was the progress toward modernization slow but these constitutional regimes faltered, giving way to various autocratic, authoritarian, or semi-authoritarian regimes.

From this point of view these developments are not entirely dissimilar from others in the history of development of modern societies. The case of the initial modernization of China, so often used as a negative example in comparison with the more successful initial modernization of Japan, comes immediately to mind.[6] Similarly, the long history of several Latin American countries, briefly described above, may come into the picture, especially when—as in Perón and post-Perón Argentina—an evident progress to modernization was halted or reversed. Lastly, the example of

---

"Revolutionary Protest Movements in Underdeveloped Areas"; and M. Brecher, "Political Instability in the New States of Asia," and R. Emerson, "The Erosion of Democracy in the New States," in H. Eckstein and D. Apter, eds., *Comparative Politics: A Reader* (New York: Free Press of Glencoe, Inc., 1963), pp. 617-44.

[5] On Indonesia, see H. Feith, *The Decline of Constitutional Democracy in Indonesia* (Ithaca, N.Y.: Cornell University Press, 1962); and W. A. Hannah, *Bung Karno's Indonesia* (New York: American Universities Field Staff, 1961). On Burma, see E. R. Leach, "L'avenir Politique de la Birmanie," *Bull Sedeis* (Paris: Futuribles, November 1962); and L. W. Pye, *Politics, Personality and Nation Building* (New Haven: Yale University Press, 1962). On Pakistan, see K. B. Sayeed, "The Collapse of Parliamentary Democracy in Pakistan," *Middle East Journal*, 8, 4 (1959), 389-406; and K. Callard, *Pakistan: A Political Study* (New York: The Macmillan Company, 1957).

[6] M. J. Levy, "Contrasting Factors in the Modernization of China and Japan," in S. Kuznets, W. E. Moore, and J. J. Spengler, eds., *Economic Growth: Brazil, India, Japan* (Durham, N.C.: Duke University Press, 1955), pp. 496-537; and G. M. Beckman, *The Modernization of China and Japan* (New York: Harper & Row, Publishers, 1963).

the rise of militarism in Japan,[7] and especially of Fascism and Nazism in Europe in the Twenties and Thirties,[8] should also be mentioned as perhaps the most important cases, at much more advanced levels of development, of breakdown of modernization—and with much more far-reaching attempts at almost total demodernization.

Another direction or outcome of such eruptions is the development and institutionalization of a new, relatively more flexible and differentiated type of modern society. The best examples of this are the various revolutionary or semirevolutionary regimes—Soviet Russia, Turkey, Mexico—or at least some of the anticolonial, nationalistic elites in the new states and in some Latin American countries. More partial examples or at least attempts at institutionalization of new types of modern regimes after periods of disorganization or blockages can be found, as we have seen, in certain Latin American and many European countries.

Throughout our analysis we shall focus on these conditions which facilitate sustained growth as against those which may lead to situations of breakdown or stagnation. We will do so because, in our view, modernity and the aspirations to modernity imply such a tendency to continuous change and pose the problem of the ability to absorb such change. But this certainly does not mean that the ability to develop institutional frameworks capable of absorbing change is given or assured or that even it constitutes the usual, "normal" outcome of processes of modernization. On the contrary it may well be that some type of more stagnating nontraditional regimes may be indeed more common than one which is fully capable of continuously absorbing change. It may well be that the conditions which lead to the development of growth-sustaining institutions do not occur frequently. It is to the analysis of these different types of conditions that we shall turn now.

Thus we are brought back to the central focus of our analysis—namely that of the conditions under which such different types of breakdown or stagnation and, conversely, institutional structures capable to assure sustained growth tend to develop.

CHARACTERISTICS OF SITUATIONS OF BREAKDOWN

In order to be able to understand more fully both the conditions and the repercussions of such breakdowns it would be worth while to analyze more fully some of their most pertinent manifestations in some of the

[7] R. A. Scalapino, "Japan between Traditionalism and Democracy," in S. Neumann, ed., *Modern Political Parties* (Chicago: University of Chicago Press, 1956); and I. Morris, ed., *Japan 1931-1945: Problems in Asian Civilizations* (Boston: D. C. Heath & Company, 1963).

[8] S. Neumann, "Germany: Changing Patterns and Lasting Problems," in Neumann, ed., *ibid.*, pp. 354-94.

major institutional spheres, both drawing on the preceding description and supplementing it through more detailed analysis of some cases.

The most general characteristic of situations of breakdown in the political sphere was a marked discrepancy between the demands of different groups and the responses and ability of the central rulers to deal with these demands.

The levels of these demands are, in such situations, either higher or lower (i.e., more or less articulated) than the level of aggregation and policy making within the central institutions. Usually in these situations the demands of most social groups oscillated continually between politically relatively highly articulated types of demands, as manifest in the formation of varied interest groups and of social movements with a high level of political intensity; and the more primitive, less articulated types of demands manifest in direct pressures on the bureaucracy in petitioning the local potentates (or bureaucracy) and central rulers and infrequent mob outbreaks.

The power position of the various groups making these varied demands has greatly increased as a result of the processes of modernization and they could no longer be suppressed and neglected, but at the same time ways were found of integrating them in some orderly way. Few middle-range institutional frameworks developed within which these varied types of political demands could become regulated and translated into concrete policy demands and policies.

The formal institutions appropriate for such aggregation and policy formulation usually existed in the form of central executive, administrative, and legislative organs on the one hand and of various parties on the other. But in their actual working these institutions were not able to perform these functions effectively.

The leadership of the parties or of the varied movements was not able to aggregate these varied interests and political orientations in some relatively ordered way or to develop adequate policies able to deal with the different demands of the major groups and with major problems to which these demands were related. Thus the most important characteristic of the political process in such situations has been not the mere existence of numerous conflicts or of different levels of articulation of demands, or even the lack of full coordination between these different levels—a situation that can easily be found in relatively stable traditional regimes. In the societies studied here, because of the push to modernization these different levels of political demands and activities were not, as in many premodern regimes, kept in relatively segregated, if interlocked compartments, but were brought into relatively common frameworks of political process and decision making. At the same time adequate mechanisms and principles of aggregating them or of regulating the conflicts attendant on their development did not develop within this framework. In other words, the new values that many people wanted to realize in these societies demanded a relatively high level of coordination of individuals' behavior, and no structure of power and organization linking these individuals with the new, more articulated demands and activities has been created—even the older structure may have broken down.

MOVEMENTS OF PROTEST

A closely related picture emerges if we examine the nature and scope of eruptions and movements of protest that have developed in these societies.

The contents of the symbols that have been developed or taken over by these movements were not necessarily different from the whole range of such symbols that has developed during different periods or stages of modernization in European, Asian, and African countries. They ranged, as we have seen, from nationalistic, anticolonial, traditionalistic, ethnic symbols, through symbols of social protest or economic deprivation, up to various symbols of cultural renovation coined in anti-Western terms or in terms of religious and communal revival. They were probably—but not necessarily—more extreme in the intensity of their protest than those that can be found in other, more sedate movements. But other more crucial characteristics of these movements and symbols stand out. One was the relative closeness, separateness, and mutual segregation of these different movements. Another was their sectarian nature, and their alternation between brief periods of highly intensive eruptions and long periods of stagnation and inactivity.

Third, within many such sectarian and mutually hostile movements there often developed—on the same level of extremist articulation—a coalescence of different, seemingly conflicting values or social orientations, such as those of traditionalism and economic development or of traditionalism and democracy. These different orientations were not usually organized or coordinated in a way that would make them meaningful in terms of the momentary situation, nor in terms of some continuous activity, policy formulation, and implementation.

This was an important indication of the lack of predisposition on the part of these various movements to become incorporated or transposed into wider frameworks, parties, or informal organs of public opinion, and of lack of adaptation to such wider regulative frameworks—often matched by the lack of ability on the part of the ruling institutions to absorb these various symbols and orientations into their own frameworks.

As a result of these characteristics, the movements of protest and opposition in these countries oscillated between apathy and withdrawal of interest of wider groups and strata from the central institutions, on the one hand, and very intensive outbursts that made extreme demands on these institutions for total, immediate change of the regime or of the place of any given groups within it.

PROCESSES OF COMMUNICATION

One characteristic of the process or structure of communication in situations of breakdown [9] has been the existence of different patterns of communication among different strata—the more traditional, closed patterns of communication within the confines of the villages and the more differentiated, sophisticated systems of the central elites or urban groups. Second, the communicative structure in these societies was often characterized by the lack of "communicative mediators" or brokers between these different levels of communicative activities. Third, it was characterized by a continual oscillation of wide groups and strata between communicative apathy toward the central institutions of the society on the one hand, and predilection to mob excitement and activity and succumbing to agitation on the other. Fourth, vicious circles of over-sensitivity to various mass media tended to develop in these societies, as well as a lack of ability to absorb these stimuli in some continuous and coherent way.

Thus here, as in the political sphere, the most important characteristic is not the mere existence of different levels or types of communication, nor even the relative weakness of some of the intermediary links between these different levels—a situation that was characteristic of many of the traditional societies. Rather, the crucial characteristic of the structure of communication in these countries was the bringing together of these different types of communicative behavior into a relatively common framework, their exposure to similar or common stimuli without the development among them of some stable patterns of receptivity.

The same situation can of course be found in the economic sphere proper. The major ills or economic problems of these societies were due not only to low levels of development of their economies, lack of available skills, or their depletion because of external events, but above all to the discrepancies between the push to modernization and the institutional ability to sustain growth, between the disruption of the traditional frameworks and the lack of possibility of finding adequate outlets in the new modernized frameworks.

Thus, in all institutional spheres we find a very similar situation—a situation of bringing together different groups, of growing interdependence and mutual awareness of these different groups, but at the same time the lack of development of adequate new common binding norms and regulative mechanisms.

[9] S. N. Eisenstadt, "Communication Systems and Social Structure: An Exploratory Comparative Study," *Public Opinion Quarterly*, 19, 2 (Summer 1955), 153-67.

CLEAVAGES BETWEEN ELITES

This inadequate development of integrative mechanisms has been manifest in several aspects of institutional development and in the sphere of crystallization of symbols.

One of the most important indications of this situation could be found in the development, in all institutional spheres—perhaps especially in the political one—of a sharp dissociation between local parochial and central leaders or cadres and "solidarity-makers" and the instrumentally task-oriented leaders and administrators.

In many of these societies a strong dissociation and rift developed between the various local (parochial)—usually more traditional, leaders—be they village, regional, or ethnic—and more modernized leaders of the emerging modern center, and there developed but few organizational and institutional settings that could bridge between them and the new emerging center.

A similar situation can be discerned in the processes of development of the new central symbols of the society in relation to those of partial groups or sectors within it. The various parochial, particularistic primordial symbols of local, ethnic caste or class groups were not incorporated into the new center of the society, and their reformulation on a new level of common identification did not take place. Of special importance here could be the possibility of a rift within the central institutions and symbols themselves—between the older state structure, based on traditional symbols, and attempts to forge out new symbols of national unity. Hence these symbols tended to become points of structural separateness and impediments for the development of a new civil order.[10]

It was not the mere persistence of these symbols that was of crucial importance, but rather the fact that they did not become incorporated into the more central symbolic framework, which had to be oriented toward the more differentiated and variegated problems that developed in these societies as a result of the continuous process of modernization and the growing interaction between the different groups within them. In other words, no new ideology or value and symbol system that could provide some minimal acceptable meaning and framework of answers to the varied problems stemming from the new social situation developed at the center.

This rift was often reinforced by a parallel one between solidarity and instrumental leaders and elites within the society.

[10] C. Geertz, "Ideology as a Cultural System," in D. Apter, ed., *Ideology and Discontent* (New York: Free Press of Glencoe, Inc., 1964); G. W. Skinner, ed., *Local, Ethnic and National Loyalties in Village Indonesians: A Symposium,* Yale University Southeast Asia Studies (New Haven: Yale University Press, 1959); and E. Shils, "Primordial, Personal, Sacred and Civil Ties," *British Journal of Sociology,* 8 (June 1957), 130-45.

This distinction is not necessarily identical with that between politicians and administrators and may well cut across them; although obviously the politicians may be more likely to become solidarity makers, while the government official may be more open to an instrumentally oriented leader. The distinction applies rather to two basic aspects inherent in any political (and social) system, although they may vary greatly in their exact structural location in different political structures.[11]

The development of such a dissociation between the two types of leaders was fully described by Feith for Indonesia,[12] but can also be found in many of the other countries studied here. In some of the new states one of these types—especially the relatively modern, efficient administrator—might have been almost entirely lacking, but even then there did develop different cadres of relatively skilled people able to organize various administrative agencies, develop new economic enterprises and some mechanisms or organs of organizational activity, and establish some policies based on these rules. Many such cadres came from the colonial administration; others developed in response to the problems of economic development or programs of educational expansion.

But in most of the cases studied here the rules, injunctions, and policies developed by these cadres, leaders, or organizations were not legitimized or upheld by new common symbols and by their leaders or groups.

The new symbols that were developed or upheld in these countries did not seem valid or relevant to the more mundane problems with which the various rules developed by the instrumental cadres were concerned. While some discrepancy between such different orientations is probably inherent in any political system, in the cases discussed here its extent was much more acute and extreme. This discrepancy can be found in all the countries studied here. Thus, for instance, in Indonesia we find that the sets of symbols and value orientations developed by Sukarno and the major parties were not only incapable of addressing themselves to the manifold problems of modernization, but negated, as it were, their existence and significance, although at the same time these problems were besetting the body politic.[13] In Burma the mixture of symbols of Buddhism and socialism developed by U Nu, especially after the first military take-over, did not deal with any but the most marginal of concrete problems besetting Burmese political life.[14]

[11] E. Shils, "Demagogues and Cadres in the Political Development of New States," in L. W. Pye, ed., *Communication and Political Development* (Princeton, N.J.: Princeton University Press, 1963), pp. 64-78.

[12] Feith, *op. cit.*

[13] *Ibid.;* and H. Feith, "Indonesia's Political Symbols and Their Wielders," *World Politics,* 16, 1 (October 1963), 79-98.

[14] F. R. Von der Mehden, "The Changing Pattern of Religion and Politics in Burma," in *Studies on Asia* (Lincoln, Nebr.: University of Nebraska Press, 1961), II, 63-73; M. Sarkisyanz, "On the Place of U Nu's Buddhist Socialism in Burma's History of Ideas," in *ibid.*, pp. 53-62; and P. E. Sigmund, Jr., *The Ideologies of the Developing Nations* (New York: Frederick A. Praeger, Inc., 1963).

In Pakistan the constitutional debates about the nature of the state in general and the Islamic state in particular did not greatly help the solution of the many acute administrative, economic, and political problems besetting this state in the first stages of its development.[15]

In Kuomintang, China, the persistence of many traditional Confucian orientations that did not undergo an internal modernizing transformation gave rise to a mixture of traditionalist orientations and symbols and more extremist antimodern or anti-Western symbols—neither of which could provide adequate guidance to many of the problems attendant on the development of modernization.[16]

The situation in some of the Latin American countries—especially Argentina in the Thirties—while differing in details from that in the new states discussed above, did exhibit some similar characteristics. There the older oligarchic elites were able to deal only to a limited extent with the new economic and political problems attendant on a continuous modernization. This limited ability and the continuously growing politicization of the broader state of the society gave rise to a constant oscillation between repressive dictators and demagogues. Each of these tried to use different types of solidary symbols. But what they usually had in common was the dissociation of these symbols from the various concrete economic, administrative, and political problems that were developing with continuous immigration, colonization, and economic development.[17]

Similarly, in Japan in the late Twenties and early Thirties the various conservative elites—be they the remnants of the older Meiji oligarchy or some of the conservative circles and new military groups—tried to uphold, in face of growing problems attendant on industrialization, some of the older general symbols of patriotism and Imperial loyalty, which were not adequate to deal with these new problems attendant on continuous industrialization and modernization.[18]

The rift between the different elites about the attitudes to modernity

[15] K. B. Sayeed, "The Collapse of Parliamentary Democracy in Pakistan," *The Middle East Journal*, 13, 14 (Autumn 1959), 389-407; and K. Callard, *Pakistan: A Political Study* (New York: The Macmillan Company, 1957).

[16] Chiang Kai-shek, *Resistance and Reconstruction: Messages During China's Six Years of War, 1937-1943* (New York: Harper & Row, Publishers, 1943); Chiang Kai-shek, *China's Destiny and Chinese Economic Theory* (New York: Roy Publishers, 1947); and H. R. Isaacs, *The Tragedy of the Chinese Revolution* (rev. ed.) (Stanford, Calif.: Stanford University Press, 1961).

[17] G. Germani, *Política y Sociedad en una época de transición* (Buenos Aires: Ed. Paidos, 1962), esp. Parts III and IV; K. Silvert, *The Conflict Society: Reaction and Revolution in Latin America* (New Orleans: Hauser, 1961); and E. de Vries and M. Echavarria, eds., *Social Aspects of Economic Development in Latin America* (Paris: UNESCO, 1963).

[18] M. Maruyama, *Thought and Behavior in Modern Japanese Politics*, ed. I. Morris (New York: Oxford University Press, Inc., 1964) and T. Ishida, *Japan's Rapid Development and Its Problems*, mimeographed.

and industrialization in pre-Fascist Italy and pre-Nazi Germany is too well known to need any further elaboration or illustration here.[19]

CONTRACTUAL ARRANGEMENTS AND
PRECONTRACTUAL SYMBOLS

If we attempt to summarize the description of the situations in the countries analyzed above, two aspects seem to stand out. First, in all the cases analyzed here, there tended to develop, in almost all the institutional spheres, a situation of growing interaction between different groups and strata, of their being drawn together into new common frameworks, of growing differentiation and at the same time lack of adequate mechanisms to deal with the problems attendant on such internal differentiation and on the growing interaction between the various groups. This coming together of different groups into common social frameworks may have been intermittent and unequally distributed between different groups and strata of the population. But from all these points of view it is extremely doubtful whether it differed greatly from developments in other modernizing or modern societies at similar levels of modernization that were more successful in establishing relatively stable institutional frameworks.

This situation could be again described in Durkheim's terms as the nondevelopment and noninstitutionalization of the precontractual elements of contracts in the society.[20]

The number of "contracts," i.e., of different spheres of interaction—be they in the field of labor relations, industrial relations, or administrative practice—in which the need for new contractual and administrative arrangements developed was very great. But very often such effective arrangements did not develop and, even when they did, adequate frameworks for the application of normative injunctions to specific situations did not; and even when contractual arrangements developed, they were not upheld by commonly shared values and orientations.

It was the combination of these characteristics that has given rise, in many cases, to what one investigator has described as the original Hobbesian state of war, i.e., to a state of internal war of all against all without the existence of any common rules that the participants consider binding.

Again, in Durkheim's terms, in all these cases there was a failure of establishment and institutionalization of new levels of solidarity, of transition from mechanic to organic solidarity, or from a level of low organic solidarity to a higher one, even though the older frameworks of solidarity

[19] Neumann, "Germany: Changing Patterns and Lasting Problems," in Neumann, ed., *op. cit.*; G. J. Magnone, "Italy," in T. Cole, ed., *European Political Systems* (New York: Alfred A. Knopf, Inc., 1961); and R. Grew, "How Success Spoiled the Risorgimento," *Journal of Modern History,* **34,** 3 (September 1962), 238-55.

[20] E. Durkheim, *The Division of Labour in Society* (New York: Free Press of Glencoe, Inc., 1947).

were undermined by the growing differentiation and interaction between the different groups.[21]

Thus in most general terms the situation that develops in such cases is one in which, despite the growing interrelation between various groups and the development of new social and cultural symbols, and despite a growing tendency to a participatory, mass-consensual society, no new viable center and no real civil order develops—a center capable of responsively regulating the problems and demands of the various groups and a civil order that combines the maintenance of some institutional arrangements with such new, broader orientations and symbols.

These various aspects of situations of breakdown did not necessarily always develop to the same degree—the dissociation between different types of elites might have been greater in some cases than the nonincorporation of traditional symbols into the modern center. Of special importance here was the relative importance of the rift between local and central institutions and symbols, which is more prominent in societies with lower levels of differentiation, as against the rift between *solidary* and *instrumental* elites and symbols, which becomes more important or crucial in situations of higher levels of social modernization.

But whatever their exact constellation, they all indicated that the emerging modern system has not been able to deal adequately with some of the basic problems of modernization. Each of the elements of such a center and such a civil order—institutional frameworks of order as manifest in legal and administrative organizations, new national symbols, orientation to some broader, more encompassing groups—do develop in these situations. However, they tend not to reinforce one another, but rather to develop in separate ways, in a way working against one another.

Thus, while some new national symbols and centers tended to develop, these national identifications were not always conceived as overriding all parochial or traditional loyalties and as encompassing them; or they were conceived, as in the cases of the more extreme populist and/or autocratic and totalitarian regimes, as negating them as well as the importance of claims of individuals and groups to dignity and social justice.

Similarly, the multiplication of different administrative and bureaucratic organization on the central and local levels was not buttressed by autonomous organs of legislation, legality, or public opinion.

Thus in all these cases the basic tendencies to consensual mass participation were either minimized, ignored, or suppressed. The exact patterns of such developments, of the various rifts in the body politic, of lack of development of a civil order, or of its deformation took on different contours in different situations.

[21] *Ibid.;* and S. P. Huntington, "Political Development and Political Decay," *World Politics,* **17** (1965), 386-430.

CHARACTERISTICS OF POLITICAL PROCESS IN SITUATIONS
OF SUSTAINED GROWTH

Insofar as the various conditions analyzed above subsist or continue—and very often they may continue for long periods of time—one of the more regressive or stagnative institutional outcomes will usually develop.

However, these conditions may also be changed—reversed, as it were—and give rise, as we have seen, to a new structural recrystallization, which may be able to develop a much greater ability for successful absorption of change, which will develop the conditions for some measure of sustained growth.

What, then, are the characteristics of the processes of relatively successful absorption of changing demands and problems, as contrasted with those of breakdown and stagnation?

The most crucial aspect of a relatively successful absorption of such different demands is the extent to which they are more or less successfully aggregated or subsumed under some wide, stable, and flexible policies and organizations; i.e., the extent to which discrete interests are subsumed into some broader frameworks and the more totalistic orientations of the various social movements are abated.

Such process entails, of course, the development of the features that characterize situations of breakdown—i.e., the minimization of cleavages between instrumental and solidary elites, the growing incorporation of various partial symbols in the central symbols of the society, and above all, the growing integration of political activities of different interest groups and social movements into more stable frameworks, the acceptance of common rules of the political game, and the development of adequate, binding, regulatory norms and mechanisms.

The focus of all these activities is inevitably the process of absorption of demands of various groups into the central institutions of the system.

The establishment of such a *modus vivendi* greatly depends, first, on the integration of different types of interest groups and social movements in the wider framework of different parties, or other groups which perform such functions. The nature of such integration varies greatly between different types of regime and at different stages of their development.

Second, it depends greatly on the ways in which the different concrete issues which constitute the focuses of protest or dispute are dealt with.

The most important way of dealing effectively with these problems is, of course, the crystallization and implementation of some policies that can, at least to some extent, accede to the demands of different groups and deal with the problems from which these demands stemmed.

Thus, for instance, the development of various socio-economic policies such as factory laws, social security schemes, and progressive taxation on free education could to some extent deal with the economic problems and demands of many groups that developed with growing differentiation. The extension of political rights to wider groups or categories alleviated the potential extremism of demands for full participation in the political sphere. Similar illustrations could of course be found in many other fields.

But such policies have rarely completely satisfied all the demands of all the groups—especially as the accedance to the demands of one group very often meant denial of demands of other groups.

The crucial test of relatively successful absorption of change and of dealing with continually emerging problems has therefore been the extent to which such policies were implemented in such a way that even the losing groups were not entirely deprived of some of their positions and of their feeling of belonging to the society, were not entirely alienated from it, and could still maintain some positive orientations to its central institutions and symbols.

The acceptance by both the rulers and the various social strata and groups of the principles and of the implementation of such policies was to a very great degree dependent also on at least partial incorporation and legitimation of some of the symbols of protest into the central symbolic spheres of society; as, for instance, ideals of social justice, of universal citizenship, or of social rights were incorporated in various modern constitutions.[22]

Such incorporation of the various symbols and demands of various groups has rarely been complete in the sense of either full acceptance or legitimation of the protest symbols and orientation, or of negating or entirely obliterating the protest element within them. This is true of the protest of both the left and the right. However great the legitimation of the demands for equal political participation, for social justice, and for economic rights in various western European countries, in none of them did they come to deny entirely either the more traditional, regional, or even estate symbols of national unity or some other, more liberal, individualistic rights.

True, the successful implementation of these policies and incorporation of various symbols into the central sphere of the society did not impede the development of more extremist orientations, whether on the left or right or of populist variety. Such orientations did develop continuously in a relatively articulated way among various small literary groups, and in a more diffuse way among wider groups of the population.

However incomplete such process of absorption was, it did abate many

[22] S. H. Beer and A. B. Ulam, eds., *Patterns of Government: The Major Political Systems of Europe* (New York: Random House, Inc., 1962).

of the discrete, separate, and/or potential totalistic demands and orientations, and made possible some partial acceptance of these orientations and symbols and their transformation into more regular and stable elements of the political process.

Of crucial importance here has been the extent to which these different policies were successful in segregating the various social problems, such as education, urban renewal, etc., from becoming fused with more central political and cultural symbols. The more successfully separated these two aspects have been, the greater on the whole has been the absorption of the various protest orientations within the central institutional frameworks.

All these factors facilitated the development, in such situations, of a viable civil order within the framework of the new symbols and central institutions—although even here, as we have seen above, many concrete differences of course existed between the major regimes within which some such ingredients of the civil order developed.

We now come back to the question or problem posed earlier—what are the conditions of sustained growth as against conditions of breakdown or stagnation? The preceding analysis indicates that these conditions are not simply related to any of the socio-demographic or structural indices of modernization.

Although, obviously enough, some minimal development within a society of these indices can be seen as a necessary condition for the development of any modern structure, the further extension of these indices does not necessarily assure the continuous extension of modernization, the creation of a viable political or social structure capable of sustained growth, of dealing with new social, economic, and political problems.[1]

Admittedly, without some minimal degree of social mobilization and structural differentiation no modernization is possible. One cannot envisage a modern economy without the development of markets, labor, capital, and demand for the products of industry, without some

[1] K. W. Deutsch, "Social Mobilization and Political Development," *American Political Science Review,* **55** (September 1961), 494-95; United Nations, *Report on the World Social Situation* (New York, 1961); and S. N. Eisenstadt, "Modernization and Conditions of Sustained Growth," *World Politics,* 16, 4 (July 1964), 576-94.

CHAPTER SEVEN

Preliminary Conclusions: Conditions of Breakdown and of Sustained Growth

degree of urbanization. Similarly, one can scarcely envisage a modern political system without some administrative centralization, and without the tendency of wider groups ar.d strata to participate in the political process and of the rulers to influence or control this participation. Also, the extension of criteria of universalism and achievement, and of growing specialization, into strategic parts of the social structure—especially in the sphere of social stratification and the legal system—constitute a crucial precondition of any process of modernization.

But beyond these minimal conditions the picture is certainly much more complex. In many cases—such as several central and eastern European, Latin American, and Asian countries—a negative correlation has developed at certain levels between a high degree of development of various socio-demographic indices, such as the degree of literacy and the spread of mass media of formal education or of urbanization, and the institutional ability to sustain growth.

Thus the implicit assumption that existed in many of these studies (that the less traditional a society is, the more it is capable of such sustained growth) has been disproved. The various socio-demographic or structural indices of modernization indicate only the extent to which traditional, self-contained societies or communities become weakened or disintegrated; the extent to which (to paraphrase the title of Dan Lerner's book) traditional society is passing.[2] But they do not in themselves indicate the extent to which a new, viable, modern society capable of such continuous growth may develop, or exactly what kind of society will develop, what its exact institutional contours will be.

A similar picture can be found with regard to the structural variety attendant on modernization. The types of structural differentiation that have taken place as a result of processes of modernization certainly were not always of the type predominant in the West during its own initial stages of modernization; that is, they did not always take the form of a continuous growth of different collectivities with specialized functions in the economic, political, and cultural fields, of seemingly continuous expansion of universalistic and achievement criteria in all these institutional spheres, and concomitant receding of particularistic relations in all spheres of life.

Similarly, the interrelationship between economic and political development has proved to be rather complicated and paradoxical. Contrary to the rather naive assumption often found in the older literature that these two are always concomitant and reinforce one another, more recent evidence shows that, at least in somewhat later stages of modernization, they might sometimes run counter to each other. The main contradictions may be seen in the fact that growing political modernization cre-

[2] D. Lerner, *The Passing of Traditional Society* (New York: Free Press of Glencoe, Inc., 1958).

ates demands and pressures for various benefits that may undermine economic development, while rapid economic development may enhance the power of various traditional or neotraditional groups who may be opposed to the modern political framework.

The explanation of breakdowns in terms of intensification of conflicts or economic depression has also been proved not to be adequate. It is true, of course, that such conflicts did develop in these countries and that the existing political leadership was unable to deal with them. But why was that so? It is not the very existence of such conflicts or of bad economic conditions that is of crucial importance. Conflicts or economic problems of what initially seemed alarming magnitudes probably did exist, and have been resolved, even if only partially, in other modern or modernizing countries. What, therefore, *is* of crucial importance is the fact that in such situations these conflicts were not resolved or regulated, and that because of this they spiralled into a series of vicious circles that undermined the very stability and continuity of the emerging modern frameworks.

INTERRELATIONS BETWEEN ELITES AND BROADER STRATA

Can we, then, find some explanations of conditions of breakdown as against conditions of growth through the analysis of some of the other variables we have used in the analysis of patterns of modernization?— the modernizing orientations of different elites, the relations between these innovating groups and the broader strata and institutional settings within which they operate, the temporal sequence of modernization.

The importance of these interrelations is inherent in the very process of modernization. Such process is dependent not only on the push given by the elites that develop goals of modernization, but also on the extent to which the major types of resources needed for the working out and the maintenance of modern institutions, organizations, and activities are produced by different social strata; by the extent to which such strata are able to regulate the problems attendant on the development of the processes of differentiation through which these resources are created; and by the extent to which they are able to provide resources to the various modernizing elites. The relations between such self-modernization of different groups and strata and between the modernizing efforts of various elite groups inevitably greatly influence the development of types of political demands by these various strata, the extent of resources created by them, and the political self-perception of the strata and elites alike—their mutual perception of the crucial problems of modernization, and the ability of the elites to solve them.

Among the aspects of this interrelationship between the different elites and the broader social structure the most important from the point of view of sustained growth seem to be, first, the general level of development of internal modernization of the different strata that take part in the process of modernization, and the general level of resources that are generated by them in this process. Second is the extent to which the various strata are able to develop various autonomous regulative mechanisms and provide resources for the process of modernization. Third is the extent of compatibility or affinity between the modernizing elites and the major social strata. Fourth is the interrelationship between different elite groups, especially the extent of harmony or dissociation between the more technical, professional, and administrative elites, on the one hand, and the more generalized, solidarity-making political and cultural elites on the other.

Insofar as there exists some affinity, even if it is rather passive, between the modernizing elite or elites and the major groups and strata, and among the major modernizing elites, the process of political modernization is smooth with relatively few far-reaching eruptions.

Similarly, the stronger and more cohesive internally are the major strata, and the more they are able to participate in the process of modernization in various institutional spheres, the greater is the extent of resources that they are able to put at the disposal of various modern institutions and organizations. The greater too is their ability to regulate, through some autonomous mechanism, some of the problems attendant on the growing differentiation and modernization, to articulate realistic political demands, and to influence the formulation of major political goals and policies by the elites.

In more general terms it seems that relatively continuous progress and institutionalization of modernization in general, and political modernization in particular, tends to be greater insofar as the modernizing elites are relatively strong and cohesive and can mobilize adequate support from different strata, without by this very process giving rise to new cleavages within the society and undermining the cohesion of the major strata.

Insofar as such conditions obtain there develop, within any such modern or modernizing society, both what has been designated earlier in Durkheim's term as "contractual" and "precontractual" frameworks, and different elites which, while concentrating more in contractual (administrative, technical, or economic) and the precontractual (cultural, political, and professional) spheres, do not become too dissociated and antagonistic.

What, however, are the conditions that facilitate the development of these characteristics of various elites and strata and of their interrelations?

The preceding analysis of continuous modernization on the one hand, and of situations of breakdown on the other, indicates that the successful absorption of potential orientations of protest is both highly contingent on and results in the development of a relatively flexible institutional structure—the flexibility of which can best be seen in the bringing together of relatively differentiated interests in the coexistence within relatively common frameworks of highly different types of social and political orientations, and in the development of differentiated levels of consensus and of procedural rules of solving conflicts. Such flexible institutional structure may perform very important functions of socializing the new groups that were continuously drawn into the central political institutions, of reinforcing and sustaining among different groups, positive orientations to modernization, and sometimes even of facilitating their development.

STRUCTURAL FLEXIBILITY: THE POLITICAL FIELD

We shall examine the major manifestations of such flexibility in two major spheres of the social order—the political sphere and the broader sphere of social organization.

In the political sphere the existence and development of such flexibility depend on certain combinations between the innovative and the more conservative aspects of political institutions.[3]

The various case studies analyzed above indicate that, while impetus to political change and innovation can be located in all the different types of political organizations and institutions, some forms of political organizations seem to be especially likely to become the force of such innovations and of the institutionalization of political change. One arena of political innovation is the political party, especially one that developed from a social movement and within which different interest groups are integrated, through the activities of a central political leadership and elite. The leaders of such parties are often committed to some goals or change, and they have to attempt to mobilize broad support and to integrate different interest groups and broader public opinion so as to assure the maximization of such support.

Another impetus to change and political innovation may come from independent leadership and public opinion, ranging from relatively organized political leadership and social, political, professional, and cultural elites to different types of more diffuse public opinion.

While such leadership may be found in any and every form of political organization, it tended to direct at least some of its activities and

[3] C. J. Friedrich, *Constitutional Government and Democracy* (rev. ed.) (New York: Blaisdell Publishing Co., 1950); H. Finer, *The Theory and Practice of Modern Government* (New York: John Wiley & Sons, Inc., 1962), esp. Parts I, II; and S. N. Eisenstadt, "Political Modernization: Some Comparative Notes," *International Journal of Comparative Sociology*, **5**, 1 (March 1964), 3-24.

innovating impulses to parties and to representative-legislative frameworks.

The other major political organizations and institutions—the executive and the bureaucracy—usually tend, unless they are closely related to leadership (which in certain stages of modernization may develop out of the more traditional executive) or to parties, to be more conservative; that is, less likely to be seedbeds of political innovation—although when connected with such leadership they may easily develop considerable innovating activities.

However, the institutionalization and absorption of such changes and innovations are greatly dependent on the degree to which the innovating groups and organizations become closely related to the executive and bureaucracy and are able to develop such frameworks and work within them.

The bureaucracy and the executive provide some of the indispensable frameworks for the provision of administrative services to the various groups and strata in the population, for the regulation of political processes and for the maintenance of political frameworks. Moreover, as the executive usually serves as the symbol of the political community, it also plays a very important part in the assurance of the continuity of the political system.

Hence, the possibility of some continuous institutionalization of political innovation and of absorption of changing political demands and organizations, which constitutes, as we have seen, the crucial test of political modernization, is greatly dependent on the extent to which these frameworks function in a stable way and some continuous and viable *modus vivendi* between them and the more innovating organizations and agencies can be established.

The establishment of such a *modus vivendi* depends greatly on the integration of different types of interest groups and social movements in the wider framework of different parties or other groups that perform such functions. On the other hand, the establishment of such a *modus vivendi* between the different political institutions greatly facilitates the ability of the political elites to effect some integration of interests and social movements within the framework of political parties or partylike organizations.

Such flexibility and capacity for absorption are not necessarily tied to just one type of structural variety or organization and can be found, as we have seen, under many different types of structural arrangements, such as multiparty or single-party regimes and small-scale or large-scale (bureaucratic) organizations. The concrete nature of such integration and subsumption of varied interests and demands under some general principles of policy varies greatly between different types of regimes and at different stages of their development, but some such integration of diverse political interests and activities and organization within the frameworks of "party-political" activities constitutes a basic prerequisite of the institutionalization of any modern political system.

RIGIDITY AND FLEXIBILITY OF STATUS SYSTEMS

The development of a modern institutional structure that facilitates the development of cohesive strata with positive orientations to modernization is dependent not only on the crystallization of some characteristics of the political structure, but also on the development of certain flexibility within the broader social structure—and especially in those of its aspects which serve as interlinking mechanisms between the central societal institutions, the emerging modern center, and the broader social strata; the periphery. The continuous absorption of change necessarily entails the development of social processes which tend on the one hand to break up any fixed, freezing ascriptive arrangements of groups and power structure, while on the other hand they facilitate the continuous restructuring of the distribution of power, wealth, and prestige and the rearrangement of different social groups and roles within common institutional frameworks.[4]

Of crucial importance here is the extent of development of flexibility of the status system, as evident in the autonomy and mutual openness of various elites and social groups, in terms of their status symbols.

Perhaps the clearest illustration of such autonomy and of status orientations is found among many of the Protestant groups, which, as we have seen above, were among the initial modernizers in western Europe.[5] They evinced, as we have seen, a combination of two characteristics or orientations. First was their openness toward the wider social structure, rooted in their "this-worldly" orientation which was not limited to the economic sphere but extended gradually into demands for wider political participation and for setting up of new, wider political frameworks and criteria. The Protestant groups were characterized second by a certain autonomy and self-sufficiency from the point of view of their status orientation.

Some ingredients of such autonomy can be found, as we have seen, in different forms in many other societies.

Such relative autonomy and flexibility of status orientation tends to influence greatly the interrelation between different groups and strata.

---

[4] S. N. Eisenstadt, *Essays on the Sociological Aspects of Political and Economic Development* (The Hague: Mouton, 1961), esp. pp. 49-53.

[5] M. Weber, *The Protestant Ethic and the Spirit of Capitalism*, trans. T. Parsons (New York: Charles Scribner's Sons, 1958); R. H. Tawney, *Religion and the Rise of Capitalism* (New York: Harcourt, Brace & World, Inc., 1926); and H. Trevor-Roper, "Religion, the Reformation and Social Change," *Historical Studies*, 4 (1965), 18-45.

It may enable the development of some new status criteria and groups without great disruption of the cohesion of the older groups. It may greatly facilitate the development of new elites willing to learn new modern roles in the economic, organizational, and political spheres.

Such new elites (or the members of the old elite that have learned new tasks and patterns of behavior) can often acquire an established place in the structure of the societies, and so find some sort of *modus vivendi* with the older ones. The new criteria of status (i.e., of economic achievement and specialization, of participation in a political party or youth movement) often overlap with many of the older traditional ones without creating close groups constituted only according to one type of criterion, and in this way enable a relatively continuous development of varied organizations within a relatively common structure.

In many cases the new groups not only have access to existing social positions, but new types or symbols of wealth, power, and prestige and of channels of access to major social positions can develop and the relative position of different groups with regard to all of them may change continuously.[6]

The concrete structural constellations of such status flexibility are numerous and certainly are not limited to any particular type, such as the type developed in Western societies. Thus, the situation in Japan, where we have seen a continuous development, almost segmentation, of new particularistic units—economic corporations, cliques, or neighborhood groups—together with some differentiation between the occupational, political, and community fields, or the attempts in Russia to break down the ascriptive tendencies of the upper echelons of the society, are interesting manifestations of different concrete structural developments of such status flexibility.[7]

But the existence of such openness and status flexibility is not assured at any level of social differentiation and modernization; nor is it assured by the mere extension of social mobilization. As we have seen above, contrary tendencies to particularistic-ascriptive closure and freezing of different groups and organizations may develop on every level of complexity or of differentiation. And while obviously the extension of social mobilization and differentiation is a *necessary* condition for the development of modernization, it is the extent to which such extension will foster openness and status flexibility that will assure the conditions sufficient for the sustained growth as against breakdown.

Both such status flexibility and the opposite tendencies to ascriptive

---

[6] Eisenstadt, *Essays, op. cit.*

[7] E. Vogel, *Japan's New Middle Class* (Berkeley, Calif.: University of California Press, 1963); R. Feldmesser, "Towards a Classless Society?" in A. Inkeles and K. Geiger, eds., *Soviet Society* (Boston: Houghton Mifflin Company, 1961), pp. 573-82; and N. De Witt, "Upheaval in Education," *Problems of Communism*, 7 (January 1959).

freezing of structural arrangements can be found in all spheres of social organizations—in political parties, labor organizations, different areas and channels of mobility—and are not necessarily tied to any specific structural form or level of development. Similarly, they may occur within seemingly similar social groups or strata, be they upper aristocratic, various middle strata such as entrepreneurs, professional groups, or workers' groups or organizations.

The development of such status flexibility is closely related to the relative predominance, in modern societies, of universalistic *versus* particularistic criteria within different groups, and especially in the regulation of relations between them.

Within any group, community, or organization that develops in modern society many particularistic, ascriptive, and diffuse orientations inevitably tend to persist and develop. Thus on the local community level the ties of friendship, often kinship and common residence, have many particularistic and ascriptive orientations that are perpetuated and often even restructured in modern settings.[8] Similarly, *within* any organization, however specifically oriented, many such particularistic and ascriptive orientations and relations also tend to develop in the form of various primary groups, or through such organizations' attempts to extend the scope of their activities and to acquire some "monopolistic" positions within a community.[9] Even on the symbolic, and to some extent legal level of the central community many such particularistic orientations tend to develop.[10]

The extent of the openness and flexibility of any modern society is dependent not on the *total* erosion of particularistic ties, but on their specific structural placement with regard to the more universalistic ones, and especially on the extent of prevalence of criteria of universalism and achievement in the various interlinking spheres and mechanisms between the different groups, strata and institutional spheres, in the regulation of access to them, in the extent of general mobility in the society and of the possibility of continuous crystallization of new units which go at any stage beyond the given situation and balance of power.

This conclusion entails a basic reformulation of the usual approach to the problem of the relation between degrees of traditionalism and success in adaptation to modern conditions. The preceding analysis indi-

[8] S. N. Eisenstadt, "Bureaucracy, Bureaucratization, Markets and Power Structure," *Essays in Comparative Institutions* (New York: John Wiley & Sons, Inc., 1965), pp. 175-216.

[9] Eisenstadt, *ibid.;* and T. Parsons, *System and Process in Modern Societies* (New York: The Free Press, 1960), esp. part II.

[10] T. Parsons, *Societies in Comparative and Evolutionary Perspectives,* forthcoming; E. Shils, *Political Development in the New States* (The Hague: Mouton, 1962); W. J. Goode, *Industrialization and Family Change,* North American Conference on the Social Implications of Industrialization and Technological Change (Chicago, 1960); B. F. Hoselitz, *Sociological Aspects of Economic Growth;* and C. Kerr, *Industrialism and Industrial Man* (Cambridge, Mass.: Harvard University Press, 1960).

cates that the structural features that characterize a traditional society are not necessarily in themselves the most important determinants of the degree of adjustment or adaptation to modern conditions. The important characteristics seem to be the degree of solidarity of the family and of the community, flexibility of elites and of systems of stratification, and probably other factors, not always directly related to the basic structural "typological" characteristics of traditional societies, and more closely related to the cultural differentiation and interrelations between different subgroups that exist within the common framework of these different types of societies than to their overall structural characteristics.[11]

SOME CONDITIONS OF STRUCTURAL FLEXIBILITY

The development and continuity of such structural flexibility and of the openness of the major elites and strata can be greatly reinforced by many structural factors, institutional arrangements, processes, and conditions, the development and continuous functioning of several types of institutional arrangements. Among such institutional arrangements of special importance are the basic legal and political frameworks that guarantee the free allocation and access to institutional spheres and roles and the possibility of changing one's position through processes of mobility and recrystallization of various societal units. Educational institutions, channels of open mobility, and voluntary associations in which various groups and strata can unite and act together are perhaps the best illustrations of such frameworks beyond the political sphere. Within all these the initial patterns of establishment of central institutional modern frameworks seem to be of special importance.

The establishment and continuity of flexible political symbols and central and political and legal frameworks; of common symbols of political-national identification; and of organs of political struggle, legislation, and administration are basic prerequisites for the development of a sense of modern, differentiated political identity and affinity among different groups and strata that are drawn into the context of modern political community, and of the development of a civil order.[12]

Such institutions constitute an important agent of continuous political socialization of wider groups and strata, i.e., of their absorption into the central political sphere, of their acceptance of modification of the major rules of the political game, of the criteria of regulation of their demands, or legal rights and procedures of rules of political struggle and of allocations of administrative services.[13] Conversely, the nonde-

---

[11] Eisenstadt, *Essays in Comparative Institutions,* Part II.

[12] G. Almond, "Introduction: A Functional Approach to Comparative Politics," in G. Almond and J. S. Colemans, eds., *The Politics of Developing Areas* (Princeton, N.J.: Princeton University Press, 1960), pp. 3-64; E. Shils, *op. cit.;* and M. Lipset, *Political Man* (Garden City, N.Y.: Doubleday & Company, Inc., 1960).

[13] Lipset, *ibid.*

velopment of such frameworks may reinforce the closeness and divisiveness of the various elites and broader strata.

Insofar as such frameworks do not develop, the various characteristics of structural duality of delinquent communities and levels of intrasocietal conflicts may easily persist and even become intensified throughout growing social mobilization and differentiation. It is such persistence and not the mere nondevelopment of high levels of differentiation that is most conducive to, and characteristic of, situations of breakdown. But the effectiveness and continuity of these central symbols and institutions as agents of political socialization is not given or assured through their mere establishment. Such effectiveness and continuity are greatly dependent on several other additional factors, processes, or conditions that influence the extent to which various groups become modernized in such a way that they are able to develop both new regulative frameworks through which their problems can be dealt with, and general positive orientations to wider modern frameworks and symbols.

Several aspects of the general tempo of modernization, and the differential tempo of modernization in different institutional spheres, are very important.[14] Of great importance also is the overall continuity of economic development and progress. The greater such continuity the greater also is the positive adjustment of various groups and strata to the new, modern settings.

But of no smaller importance, because it influences the relative ability of the institutions to deal effectively with the different crises of modernization, is the relative temporal sequence of modernization in different institutional spheres. The less these different crises and problems arise at the same time, the greater is the absorptive capacity of the modern institutional system.

Similarly, such absorptive capacity is greater insofar as the frameworks that deal with regulation of conflicts are set up, and the propensity to accept regulation of conflicts develops among broader groups before the onset of intensive conflicts.

Thus, so far as the modernization of the central political institutions takes place before that of the periphery without at the same time blocking its incorporation, the greater are the chances for sustained development. Similarly, these chances are greater insofar as the internal religious and ideological transformation of social groups, on the one hand, and their integration in modern economic frameworks on the other, take place before their full politicization in terms of the development of excessive political demands. Last, the success of development of internal regulative mechanisms is greater insofar as internal values and status transformation come side by side with economic differentiation, or at least do not lag far behind it.

[14] *Ibid.*, Part I, pp. 45-178.

IDEOLOGICAL TRANSFORMATION AND COHESION OF ELITES

However, the cohesiveness and openness of various groups and strata—and especially of the elite groups, which we have found to be of crucial importance for the development of institutional flexibility—depends not only on the various broader processes analyzed above, but also on the placement of these elites and groups in the broader social frameworks, as well as on their internal transformative forces; their ideological or value transformation. Moreover, such transformation is very important for the development of commitments to the specific value-orientation of modernity as well as for the sustenance of those structural mechanisms which facilitate the development of continuous structural flexibility.

This is very much in line with Weber's classical thesis about the Protestant Ethic.[15] This thesis stresses the importance of changes in religious beliefs and values for the development of new differentiated social orientations and also, to some extent, for the institutionalization of much more differentiated value systems. The major emphasis in Weber's analysis is on the influence of such religious orientations on individuals' motivation in different institutional spheres, mainly economic and to some extent scientific.[16]

The importance of these religious values for such development was rooted first in their contents, i.e., in the fact that they stressed growing transcendentalism, individualism, and growing differentiation between the secular and the more sacred spheres, and in the impact of this content on the motivation and action orientation of the individuals. But it was also rooted in the structural location of the groups that developed these orientations—in the fact that they were secondary elites, mostly organized in open sects, concentrating on economic and cultural activities that were able to spread those orientations both upward toward the central political framework, and downward toward wider groups and strata of the population.

Moreover, these orientations developed and became first institutionalized in societies that very early developed a sense of national unity, and in which nationalism itself did not become a focus of cultural innovation.

It is probably the combination of the contents of these value orientations and the structural placement of the innovating groups that has greatly facilitated the institutionalization of some status-flexibility within

[15] Weber, *op. cit.* For a collection of the discussions on this theme, see R. W. Green, ed., *Protestantism and Capitalism: The Weber Thesis and Its Critics* (Boston: D. C. Heath & Company, 1959); and S. N. Eisenstadt, ed., *Religious Transformation and Modernity: The Protestant Ethic Thesis in Comparative Perspective* (New York: Basic Books, Inc., 1967).

[16] Tawney, *op. cit.*; Trevor-Roper, *op. cit.*; and S. A. Burrell, "Calvinism, Capitalism and the Middle Classes: Some Afterthoughts on an Old Problem," *Journal of Modern History*, 32 (1960), 129-41.

the new, developing frameworks, and the development of what may be called a value and ideological transformation of a society. Such transformation provided not only the motivation for the undertaking of new activities but also the symbolic expressions and meaning for the new emerging differentiated social structure.[17]

In none of the other societies do we find a situation similar to that in western Europe and the United States, where the pattern of initial modernization was characterized by a situation in which secondary elites, the major bearers of modern attitudes, were most active in the economic and cultural spheres, and where the wider social groups and strata were to a very great extent open to these modernizing influences and tendencies in both economic and ideological spheres and were gradually drawn into the newly emerging wider economic and cultural frameworks and into the orbit of the new central political institution.

Moreover, in most of these cases a situation developed in which nationalism itself became a focus of cultural innovation and in which similar new religious or value orientations did not develop within secondary elites.

Hence in all these cases the elites faced the problem of opening up, encouraging, and regulating whatever more modernizing forces existed within the broader strata. But the extent to which their own ideological orientations helped or hindered them in the development of these activities varied greatly, with these elites' placement in the broader social structure.

Here we may distinguish between the "growth-stimulating" and "stagnative" secular ideologies [18]—between those modernized (nationalistic, political, or social) elites and ideologies which, while creating new symbols and political frameworks, were not able to effect within their respective societies any structural transformation that would facilitate continuous growth, and the elites of Mexico, Turkey, Japan, and the first modernizing elites of western Europe, which were relatively more successful in effecting such changes and transformations.

These last elites aimed in the ideological and value spheres at the development of new, more flexible sets of symbols and collective identity which, while not negating the traditional elements in their culture, could incorporate them into these new symbolic frameworks. They aimed at the transformation of the internal values of wider social groups and strata and at the development among these groups of new, more flexible orientations.

As against the above orientations we find among the elites in the other countries a certain "closure," a ritual emphasis on certain specific

[17] Trevor-Roper, *ibid.*; and Burrell, *ibid.*
[18] S. N. Eisenstadt, "Breakdowns of Modernization," *Economic Development and Cultural Change*, **12**, 4 (July 1964), 345-67.

and very limited types of status. These usually did not contain any "transcendental" or broadly universalistic orientations, their internal ideological and value transformation was relatively weak, and they tended to view the national collectivity in terms of exclusive, limited values and symbols of status, often derived from the preceding social structure. Hence they tended also to limit their own field of perception and the scope of their own activities.

Moreover, they often emphasized the total identity between different orientations of protest—social, national, and cultural—thus minimizing the flexibility of the symbols developed by them.

In these cases there usually occurred a great upsurge of strong motivations toward achievements of new modern goals and amenities, without the development of either the discipline necessary for the implementation of these goals or the norms to regulate the new varied activities, while the central institutions were, in no small measure because of the above-mentioned characteristics of this ideological orientation, too weak to effect such transformation.[19]

These different tendencies of the elites were to no small degree dependent on their placement within the emerging social structure, although the exact relation between the two is still to be explored systematically in detail.

In most of these countries the elites were mostly composed of intellectuals who in many cases constituted the only initially available modern elite.[20] They had very few internal social and ideological contacts with either the bearers of pre-existing traditions or with the wider groups of the society, and consequently but little ability to establish a strong internal cohesiveness and strong ideological and value-identifications and connections with other, potentially modernized groups and strata.

Similarly, in many of the Latin American countries, the various political elites or leaders, whether oligarchic or demagogic, were also most dissociated from the various broader groups that were continually coming into the society or impinging on its central institutions. The process of selection and formation of these elites was relatively rigid and restricted, bringing in relatively weaker elements and intensifying their alienation from the broader group as well as their internal insecurity and lack of cohesion.

The elites in Turkey, Japan, or Mexico, or some of the more cohesive elites in countries of earlier phases of modernization, were not usually

[19] D. Lerner, "Towards a Communication Theory of Modernization," in L. Pye, ed., *Communication and Political Development* (Princeton, N.J.: Princeton University Press, 1963).

[20] H. T. Benda, "Non-Western Intelligentsias as Political Elites," in J. H. Kautsky, ed., *Political Change in Underdeveloped Countries* (New York: John Wiley & Sons, Inc., 1962), pp. 235-51.

composed only of intellectual groups, but were already placed in secondary elite positions in the pre-existing structure, and had some positive orientations to the center and to other, broader social groups and strata.

In many ways it was the emergence or nonemergence of such elites that proved to be the crucial element that could facilitate or impede the crystallization in situations of social differentiation and mobilization of the structural conditions conducive to the development of a flexible institutional structure, and could greatly influence the extent of continuity of modernization or of its breakdown. Perhaps the best way to illustrate this is through a brief analysis of different patterns of breakdowns.

FORMATION AND ORIENTATIONS OF ELITES IN SITUATIONS OF BREAKDOWN

In most of the new states the major points of breakdown were focused on the rifts between the traditional local or parochial and the more modern settings, and within the modern settings themselves. The various traditional sectors in Burma, Pakistan, or Indonesia—and before that of post-Imperial China—have been continually drawn into more differentiated and modern sectors. Even those groups which remained within the older, traditional settings very often became disorganized, and large parts of their population were withdrawn from effective participation within them. Yet many of their older frameworks, symbols, and traditions of solidarity tended to persist and exert some pull and influence both in the more traditional and the more modern settings.

Within the more modern new centers the processes of disorganization and conflict continued and many new rifts developed, but even there many groups were still relatively oriented to some of the symbols of traditional solidarity. Hence the various elites could to some extent draw on the reservoirs of this traditional solidarity, and their antimodern tendencies and orientations were to no small degree tempered by the attempts to find some *modus vivendi* between modernity and traditionalism.

The situation in Argentina was already different. Throughout the last three decades of the nineteenth century and the first two of the twentieth there developed, through continuous immigration and colonization, different new relatively modern groups, such as new planters, workers, etc. These groups tended, on the whole, to be socially and culturally rather separate. However, because of the continuous economic expansion in a colonisatory set-up they were able to maintain their separate existence and mutual closeness together with continuous development, change, and modernization. They became interwoven into a closer framework of mutual interdependence only gradually. At the same time, the major oligarchic elites which held the ruling positions in the country did not develop new symbols, institutions, and policies capable of dealing with these new problems and basically maintained the framework developed in the mid-nineteenth century, thus also impeding the full integration of these groups into new, more modern frameworks.

It was only when the interrelation between these groups became closer and the continued economic expansion halted that the shaky coexistence was broken down, giving rise to long periods of conflicts and tension in the thirties, combining populist and nationalistic tendencies, then giving rise to the Peronist regime and later continuing some of the same institutional instabilities.

Thus, in a way, the case in Argentina shows the limits of the continuity and stability of a society in which precontractual elements were weak or underdeveloped from the very beginning, and which did not have any strong pre-existing traditional base of solidarity. Hence the new symbols and orientations developed by the various groups and by the various political leaders were much less anchored in common traditional backgrounds. Although many of these leaders attempted to develop some symbols of demodernization, they were limited by the various separate traditions of the different groups, by the lack of common symbols of identification against which it was possible to rebel, and by the basically positive attitudes of most of these groups toward modernization. Hence the regimes that tended to develop here were based more on vague populistic symbols and various attempts to raise the populations' participation in the central political life and its share in the economic benefits of this life, than on outright demodernization.

The situation in Japan in the Twenties and Thirties after the breakdown of the original Meiji oligarchic modernization was already couched in many terms of outright demodernization. But its potential drift to such demodernization was tempered by the persistence of the Imperial symbolism and of many traditional elements within the society, and by the relative internal weaknesses of the military cliques.

The trend toward complete demodernization has attained its peak in the development of Nazi Germany, and to a somewhat smaller extent in Fascist Italy. There it was mostly groups that attained a relatively high level of modernization that were drawn into even more new but unstable differentiated conditions. Their conflicts were set almost entirely in terms of highly differentiated interests and within frameworks of modern institutions. Whatever traditional symbols were used, they were mostly of a purely negativist, demodernizing nature, no longer being really rooted in any traditional solidarity or identification.

As against these various possibilities of stagnation and of breakdowns there are the different types of sustained growth which have been analyzed above. Both—breakdowns and the possibility of sustained growth—are inherent in the processes of modernity. They indicate the pitfalls, problems, and challenges of modernity—and the fact that modernity constitutes perhaps the greatest challenge that mankind has posed for itself in the course of its history.

Africa, 1, 2, 19, 35, 110ff
  youth movements, 30
Age, 23, 24
Agriculture, agrarian reform, 77ff, 88, 91, 92, 100-1, 108 (see also specific countries, regimes)
"Alienation," 34
"Allocation," 9-10
Argentina, 89, 94, 96-97, 132, 139, 159-60
Asia, 1, 2, 35, 44, 110ff
  first phase, 52
  youth movements, 30
  See also specific countries
Australia, 1-2
Autocratic regimes, 39
  first phase, 68ff, 69-71
  See also specific countries

Bismarck, Otto von, 69-70
Bolivia, 98
Brazil, 97
Breakdown:
  characteristics of, 133-42
  possible outcomes of eruption, 131-33
  preliminary conclusions on, 145-61
  situations of, compared with those of sustained growth, 129-61
  ubiquity of eruptions, 129-30
  See also Protest; specific causes, countries, societies
Broad status groups, 147-49
  and basic characteristics, 9
  See also Mass aspect; Status systems; specific groups
Bureaucratic systems, 60-61, 72ff, 150
  See also countries; regimes
Burma, 116, 127, 138, 159

Canada, 1-2
Castro, Fidel, 98
Chile, 97
China, 2, 99, 106, 132, 139
"Civic education," 28
Class structure, 44-45 (see also Social strata; Status systems; specific countries, societies)
Collectivities, 43-44 (see also specific countries)

Colonial societies, 35, 110-28
  characteristics of centers, periphery, 116-18
  differences among new states, 124-28
  initial modernizing, 109-11
  problems of integration, 120-28
  stratification and ideology, 118-19
  transformation of attitudes, 115-16
  unbalanced change, 111-15
  See also New states; specific countries
Communication, 87, 91, 101, 136
Communist regimes, 98-99
  characteristics of, 105-7
  See also specific countries
Consensual mass tendencies, as basic characteristic, 15-16
  See also Mass aspect
Contractual arrangements, 140-41
Cooperatives, 116
Cuba, 98
Cultural sphere, 21
  and basic characteristics, 4-5
  first phase, 52, 54
  protest in, 31-35 (see also Protest)
  See also Breakdown; Growth; specific countries, phases, societies
Crime, 24, 26

Decision making, 60-61, 73, 107, 134 (see also specific countries, regimes)
Delinquent communities, 66, 131, 132, 155
Democracy, democratization, 4 (see also Pluralistic regimes; specific countries)
Demographic-ecological sphere, 7 (see also specific areas)
Deutsch, Karl, 2
Di Tella, T. S., 95
Dominions, 1-2, 55ff (see also Canada, specific countries)
Drop-outs, 29

Economic sphere, 44, 50, 136, 146-47
  and basic characteristics, 3-4, 5
  and breakdown (see Breakdown)
  first phase, 57, 62, 64ff (see also specific countries, regimes)
  and starting points for diversity, 46-47
  and youth problems, 29
  See also Breakdown; Growth; specific countries, societies

INDEX

Educational sphere, 79-80
  and basic characteristics, 12, 16-18
  first phase, 62
  and social policy, 26
  and youth problems, 29-30 (*see also* Students)
  See also Students; specific countries, regimes
Elections, 39
Elites, 42, 137-40*ff*, 147-49*ff*, 159-61
  and basic characteristics, 9-10
  cohesion of, 156-59
  first phase, 52-53, 54*ff* (*see also* specific countries)
  and major themes of cultural protest, 34-35
  and starting points of diversity, 47-48
  See also Breakdown; Growth; Upper classes; specific elites, spheres
England, 18, 30, 35, 55*ff*
Entrepreneurial groups, 57, 58 (*see also* specific countries, types)
Eruptions (*see* Protest)
Europe, 18, 19, 35, 45, 133
  eastern, 1, 19, 44, 71 (*see also* specific countries)
  first phase, 52, 54, 71
  starting points of diversity, 46-47
  western, 1, 18, 44-45, 52, 55-67, 151, 157 (*see also* specific countries)
  youth, 27, 30
Executive, 60, 61, 107, 116, 150

Family, 3, 22-23, 78
Fascism, 133
First phase, 51-82
  absorption of change, 59-61, 73, 79-80
  autocratic regimes, 69-71*ff*
  beyond western Europe, 67-82
  protest, 61-64, 74-75
  split-up modernization, 67*ff*
  temporal sequence and structural characteristics, 58-59, 72, 78-79
  in western Europe, United States, and Dominions, 55-67
  See also specific countries
France, 18, 35, 65-67

Germany, 69-71, 74, 75, 140, 160
Gerschenkorn, A., 46-47
Growth, sustained:
  characteristics of, 142-44
  development of change-absorbing institutions, 38-43
  different starting points, 46-49
  integrative problems, 36-38
  possible outcomes of eruptions, 131-33
  preliminary conclusions on, 145-61

Growth, sustained (*cont.*)
  problems of, 36-50
  situations of, compared with those of breakdown, 129-61
  structural diversity, 43-50
  system transformation and, 40-43
  ubiquity of eruptions, 129
  See also specific countries, regimes

Halpern, M., 41
Harrison, Jane, 24
Huizinga, J., 24

Identities (*see* Cultural sphere; New states; Protest)
Ideological transformation, 156-59
India, 44, 125-27
Indonesia, 116, 127, 138, 159
Industrial revolution, 3, 21
Industrialization, 22
  first phase, 52, 53, 54, 64*ff*
  See also specific countries, regimes, spheres
Institutional spheres:
  and basic characteristics, 10
  See also specific countries, spheres
Integration (*see* Protest; Roles; Social disorganization; specific systems)
Intelligentsia, 68-69, 71, 89-90, 112, 158
  (*see also* specific countries)
Interest groups, 12-13, 59*ff* (*see also* Protest; specific countries, groups, regimes)
International aspects, 18-19
  of protest, 35
  See also specific countries
Italy, 65-67, 140, 160

Japan, 2, 44, 75-82, 133, 139, 152, 157, 158, 160
  first phase, 54
  middle classes, 45
  students, 28, 82
Juvenile delinquency (*see* Youth problems)

Kerr, C., 48
Kinship, 3 (*see also* Family)

Labor, 25-26, 86 (*see also* Trade unions; Unemployment; Workers)
Latin America, 1, 2, 19, 44-45, 84-98, 132, 133, 139, 158
  breakdowns in, 94-96
  differences among countries, 96-98
  elite formation, 90-93
  first phase, 52, 71
  initial pattern, 84-86

Latin America (*cont.*)
  structural changes, 86-90
  students, 28
  See also specific countries
Lawyers, legal profession, 77
Leftists, 33, 35, 62, 105
Legislature, 60, 61, 73, 107
Leisure time, 23-24
Louis XIV, 65

Market systems, 9, 39 (*see also* Economic sphere)
Mass aspect, culture, 15-16, 21
  first phase, 53
  See also Communication; Cultural sphere; Pluralistic regimes
Mexico, 88, 97, 98*ff*, 100, 103, 105, 157, 158
Middle classes, 44-45
  first phase, 52, 57, 65
  See also specific countries
Middle East, 19, 44
  first phase, 67, 71
  See also specific countries
Military, 78*ff* (*see also* specific countries)
Mobility (*see* Status systems; Urbanization)
Modernization, basic characteristics of, 1-19
  consensual mass tendencies, 15-16
  continuous structural differentiation, changes, 5-7
  educational field, 16-18
  international aspects, 18-19
  organizational and status systems, 7-11
  political field, 11-16
  social mobilization and social differences, 2-5

Nationalism, 18
  and breakdowns, growth (*see* Breakdown; Growth)
  See also New states; Protest; specific countries
Nation-states, 16
Nations, 16
Nazism, 133
Netherlands, 18
  first phase, 55*ff*
New states, 35, 41-42, 109-28, 138, 159
  characteristics of centers, periphery, 116-18
  differences among, 124
  initial modernizing, 109-11
  problems of integration, 120-23
  stratification and ideology, 118-19
  transformation of attitudes, 115-16

New states (*cont.*)
  unbalanced change, 111-15
  See also specific countries

Occupations:
  and basic characteristics, 3, 6
  and youth problems, 29, 30
  See also specific countries, occupations
Organizational systems:
  and basic characteristics, 7-11
  and social problems (*see* Social problems)
  See also specific countries, regimes, systems

Pakistan, 116, 127, 139, 159
Paraguay, 97
Parties, 12-13, 37, 60, 63, 82, 94-95, 149 (*see also* Protest; specific countries, spheres)
Peasants, 57, 65*ff* (*see also* Agriculture)
Pluralistic regimes, 55-67
Political parties, 12-13, 37, 60, 63, 82, 94-95, 149 (*see also* Protest; specific countries, spheres)
Political sphere, 43
  and basic characteristics, 3, 4, 5-6, 11-16
  and breakdown and growth. *See* Breakdown; Growth
  and starting points for diversity, 47
  and students (*see* Students)
  See also specific aspects, countries, organizations, spheres
Populism, 4, 25, 34-35, 63 (*see also* specific countries, regimes)
Precontractual symbols, 140-41
Pressure groups (*see* Interest groups)
Professional organizations, 39
Professions, 77
Protest, 31-35
  first phase, 61-64, 74-75 (*see also* specific countries)
  integrative problems and structural change, 36-40
  international aspects of, 35 (*see also* specific countries)
  major themes, 32
  second phase, 104-5, 107
  structural change and orientations of, 31-32
  See also Breakdown; specific countries, regimes
Protestantism, 56, 57, 58, 151, 156
Public opinion, 12-13, 13-14, 37, 73, 79, 82, 149 (*see also* specific countries, regimes, spheres)

"Radicals," 33-34

Religion, 34, 58, 61, 63, 66, 119, 135, 156, 157 (*see also* Protestantism; specific countries)

Revolutionary regimes, 98-133
structural characteristics of, 102-5
See also Revolutions; specific regimes

Revolutions, 56, 65, 71, 74 (*see also* Revolutionary regimes; specific countries)

Rightists, 33, 35, 62, 105

Roles, 43-44
separation of, 3
and social problems, 23
See also Social differences; specific roles, systems

Rulers, 39
and basic characteristics, 4
See also specific countries, regimes, spheres

Rural population (*see* Agriculture; specific countries)

Russia, 30, 69-71, 99, 100, 101, 106, 152

Savoy, House of, 65

Scandinavia, 19
first phase, 55*ff*

Second phase, 83-109
characteristics of, 83-84
colonial societies and, 109-28
Latin America and, 84-98
revolutionary-nationalist, Communist regimes and, 98-109

Secularization, 21

Semi-democracies, 4

Sex, 23, 24

Shils, Edward, 41-42, 47, 124

Social differences:
as basic characteristic, 2-5
See also Class structure; Status systems

Social disorganization, 21-35
changing pattern of youth problems, 26-31
consequences, 22-25
international aspects of protest, 35 (*see also* specific countries)
major themes of protest, 32-35
social change, structural dislocation, 21-22
social problems and social policy, 25
structural change and orientations of protest, 31-32
See also Breakdown; Protest; Structural change

Social mobilization:
as basic characteristic, 2-5
See also Social differences; Status systems

Social movements, 12-13, 37, 59, 63, 66, 73 (*see also* specific countries, regimes)

Social policy (*see* Social problems)

Social problems, 22-31, 87
changing pattern of youth problems, 26-31
and social policy, 25-26
See also Protest

Social strata, 131, 147-49 (*see also* Status systems; specific classes, countries)

South America (*see* Latin America)

Spain, 44

Split-up modernization, 68-75 (*see also* specific countries, regimes)

Status systems, 151-54
and basic characteristics, 7-11
and equality (*see* Political sphere; Protest)
first phase, 58, 59
youth and, 28
See also Class structure; Elites; Social strata; specific classes, countries

Structural change, diversity, 5-7, 20-22, 36-50, 146
and conditions of growth, 49-50
development of change-absorbing institutions, 38-43
different starting points for, 46-49
and integrative problems, 36-38
structural diversity, 43-50
and sustained growth, 36-50
system transformation, 40-43
See also Breakdown; Social disorganization; Structural flexibility

Structural flexibility, 149-55
conditions of, 154-56
and status (*see* Status systems)
See also Structural change; specific systems

Students, 27, 28, 82, 89-90 (*see also* Youth problems)

Sweden, 30

Taxation, 78, 79

"Teddy Boys," 28-29

Totalitarian systems, 4, 15-16, 39 (*see also* Communism; Revolutionary regimes; specific countries)

Trade unions, 7, 59

Tradition, 33, 42, 135 (*see also* Cultural sphere; New states; Protest; specific countries, regimes)

Transformation, 21-25
consequences of disorganization, 22-25
ideological, 156-59

Transformation (*cont.*)
  social change, disorganization, structural dislocation, 19-22
  See also Social disorganization; Structural change
Turkey, 98*ff*, 103, 104, 105, 157, 158

Unemployment, 23, 25-26 (*see also* specific countries)
United States, 1-2, 157
  first phase, 52, 55-67
Upper classes:
  first phase, 52
  See also Elites; specific countries
Urban groups, urbanization, 20, 22, 57
  and basic characteristics, 10-11
  first phase, 52, 54 (*see also* specific countries)
  social policy and, 26

Urban groups, urbanization (*cont.*)
  See also specific countries, regimes, systems

Venezuela, 97
Villages, 113 (*see also* specific countries)

Welfare state, 64
Western countries:
  first phase, 55-67
  See also Pluralistic regimes; specific countries
Westernization, 49
Working classes, 57, 59, 67 (*see also* Labor; specific countries)

Youth problems, 26-31 (*see also* Students)

Zengakuren, 28, 82